T0063329

Most of all, I would like to thank my family, my husband, Bob, my children, Shannon, Erin, Robby, Casey and TJ, for providing me with such joy and hilarity throughout the years, that I had to write it all down. Without their growing pains, I would have very little to write about. My family, however, does not stop at just my husband and children. I thank God for the family He has given me. My sisters and their husbands, my nieces and nephews, and my friends who are considered family have all played a part in making my dream a reality. Thank you all for being a part of my life.

Acknowledgements

It's funny. I had an idea, I wrote a book. It gives one such a feeling of satisfaction. Then, one tries to publish said book and you realize there is a lot more involved than you thought. Therefore, since the only thing I knew how to do was write the book, there are many people I need to thank for helping me get to this point.

Editing and proofreading were lots of fun. To that end I would like to thank all of my friends, family members and the other writer's out there who took their time to read my book and give their opinions. Thanks for being honest. I am a better writer because of them, and hopefully the book is even better then when I started it.

I would like to thank my daughter, Shannon for designing the cover of the book for me. Thank God she was given a talent for that. I think you would be a little reluctant to purchase a book with unrecognizable stick figures on the front of it.

I would also like to thank Donna Jones. Donna did the layout for the book. Donna has been a friend of mine since we were little kids and at least she has the knowledge for this type of stuff. I do not. Thanks, Donna, for all your help.

I would like to thank Trafford.com, the company through which I published this book. With their help and guidance, I was able to see my writing become an actual book. It was very exciting. Trafford could not have been more helpful. For someone just starting out in the world of writing and publishing, it was really wonderful to have someone there to help me take those first baby steps.

This book is dedicated to the memory of my parents,
Toddy and Nan Boylan,
for teaching me that a parent's love is
without boundaries, unconditional and never ending.
Thank you.

Trafford rev. 03/23/2016

 www.trafford.com
North America & international
toll-free: 1 888 232 4444 (USA & Canada)
fax: 812 355 4082

Life
Is A
Four Letter
Word

Nan Boylan Hanstein

Foreword

Life is a four letter word. I chose this title for my book because I believe life throws us many curves. It is what we choose to do with those curves that formulates our destiny. We can let it get the best of us and spend our days trying to figure out what went wrong, or we can find the amusement in it, which keeps us going. I have chosen the latter.

I was very blessed to have grown up in a household full of love and laughter. My parents were both 100% Irish. St. Patrick's Day in our house was a bigger celebration than Christmas. We ate green mashed potatoes for dinner with our corned beef and cabbage, and the house was decorated all in green, with the Clancy Brothers playing all day on the stereo. We went to church every Sunday and I attended twelve years of Catholic school.

I am often told that I get my sense of humor from my father. My father was all of five feet three inches and liked to believe he was a leprechaun. He was always the life of the party. My mother was the stable one, or so everyone thought. She had a very quiet sense of humor that most people didn't see, but my sisters and I knew that she was the one with the great sense of humor. She married my father, didn't she? My parents are gone now, and I miss them more than I ever thought possible. I think what I miss most is seeing them smile and having their loving arms around me. I know they are watching us, I feel their presence in my life all the time. I see them in my children. I find myself using their expressions. All those things my mother used to say to me and I said, "I will never say that to my children", I am now saying to my children. It is a legacy I cherish.

I met my husband Bob, we married, and started having children. Ten years later we had five children, and a very hectic household. My husband is an auto body technician (he fixes the dents), and I have made my living so far as a medical transcriptionist. It is a great career and gave me the opportunity to work from home, so I could be with the children. We couldn't afford the babysitting anyway.

It seemed at every turn there was something hilarious going on in our house. In relating these stories to other people, I heard time and time again, "You should write a book." So I did. I am turning forty this year and I guess it was about time to write it all down.

My children are wonderful little people. They are my very lifeline. I thank God for them every day. They keep things in perspective. There are times when we don't have enough money to pay the bills, the car breaks down, and things are falling apart. It is at these times that I tell myself my family is together and healthy. We have a lot of love. With that on our plates, how can we be unhappy?

Having said that, the romp through my life is, at times, one of calamity and hilarity, a journey on which I am sure I am not alone. If you look hard enough you can find amusement, lots of it, in almost any every day occurrence, from getting up in the morning until dropping in bed at night and all the times in between. It is these times, and the amusement that goes along with them, that make up the contents of my book. Hopefully you will find these situations amusing and they will make you laugh or at least smile. If I have achieved just that, then I have accomplished much more than I had hoped.

1

⟨⟩You Know Your A Mother When.....

. . . Getting up at 4:00 a.m. doesn't bother you.

. . . Kissing boo boos becomes a hobby.

. . . Your designer jeans will NOT go above your knees.

. . . Your name becomes "Johnny's mom".

. . . You don't put on rubber gloves to clean up blood. You
don't have the time; it flies fast and furious.

. . . Grocery store discount cards replace your credit cards.

. . . You cover up your tattoo for "Back to School" night.

. . . Your girlfriend calls you for a remedy for chicken pox.

. . . Your parents just smile at you now, because they "know".

. . . Your husband has put his name on a waiting list to
talk to you.

. . . It doesn't bother you to drink Pepsi with breakfast. It
may be the only meal you get that day.

. . . Going dancing three times a week gives way to
carpooling three times a week.

. . . You are in bed at 8:00 because you never know when
the next day will begin, OR, you don't get to bed before
midnight because the day has not ended yet!

. . . You refer to your husband as "dad".

. . . You now refer to your dad as "pop-pop".

. . . You are doing homework again, after being out of
school for years.

. . . You consider it an accomplishment to get all the
lunches into the right bags.

. . . You realize you could say "STOP FIGHTING" at least four
hundred times a day.

. . . Your clothes haven't seen a dry cleaner in years.

. . . You buy a maternity bathing suit, and actually wear it
in public.

. . . You call out sick from work, when you are not the one who
is sick.

. . . You don't bother putting on make-up or even combing
your hair, just to go out and get milk.

. . . You buy a housedress.

. . . You don't buy a satin blouse.

. . . Puke becomes part of your wardrobe.

. . . You become immune to the smell of poop.

. . . You are at a dinner party and you abruptly ask
everyone at the table if they washed their hands before
sitting down.

. . . You cut the crust off your sandwiches, even though you like
the crust.

. . . You hit your knees at night and thank God that you have
been given the title!!!!!!

2
◯Meet The Family

My husband Bob and I have five children. Since this book is basically about their lives and how they intertwine, or collide, with mine, I thought it best to introduce you to each one of them, and give you a little background information.

Shannon is our oldest child at 13. I love her very much. I do not however, like her. This is our first experience with a teenager and I do not like THAT either. My husband keeps asking her why she is not a straight A student, since, at home, she knows everything and we know nothing. Shannon is a gifted artist, a talent of which I am extremely jealous. I am not very artistic; I am lucky I can draw a bath on a good day. Her father has an art talent and if she had to get something from him, at least it was a talent. When Shannon came along, one would have thought that Bob and I were Adam and Eve and no one had created anything so spectacular before. For those of you who are parents, you know what I am talking about. Suddenly, we were no longer a couple, and neither one of us were individuals. We were parents. The responsibility was overwhelming. Shannon gave us a reason to be responsible. The late night dinners, coming and going as we please, spending money without thinking went out the window the day she was born. These luxuries have yet to creep back into our lives.

As with any first child in a large family, Shannon feels

burdened by the fact that she is the oldest. I wish she could remember the days when the sun rose and set on her alone. Bob and I would stare at her for hours waiting for the first "coo", that first recognition of us as mommy and daddy. When it came, we were sure we were raising another Einstein. She was the smartest, most beautiful, most precocious child on the face of the planet. We had done it! We had created the perfect human being!

Shannon was born with a cleft palate. In laymen's terms this basically means she was born without the roof of her mouth. This had to be repaired surgically when she was a year old. So, we treated her with kid gloves. We watched her sleep. We watched her eat. We watched her play. We watched her watch television. But somehow, with all that watching, we didn't see her grow up. But she did and she is every bit the teenager, trying her wings, sometimes pushing me to the limits, most times pushing me to the limits. She is a great kid. She has a heart of gold. But, she is a teenager.

We have come to refer to her in our house as Dr. Shannon and Mrs. Hyde. You never know who is going to get out of that bed in the morning. Sometimes, it is my curly-haired little girl, greeting me with "Good morning, mommy." Then there are the times that Mrs. Hyde wakes up and screams, "Why didn't you wash my blue shirt? You really want me to be the biggest dork in the whole school, don't you? Oh, and I am not watching the little guys today. I have plans with my friends." When Mrs. Hyde is around I don't even get the common courtesy of a "Good morning". I am told this is a "teenage" thing and I will just have to deal with it for the next couple of years. One of us may not live through this.

I have tried the guilt speeches, "How can you speak to me like that? Do you have any idea the sacrifices your father and I have made so that you can do whatever it is you want?" Mrs. Hyde doesn't care. She looks at me as if I was her servant. My husband says if all our kids go through the teenage years like this, we are not going to survive. The TV show Survivor has nothing on us. I would rather eat live bugs than be talked to like that. Alas, I live for the days, and there are a few, when Mrs. Hyde goes away and my little girl is there, curling up on the couch with me for a heart to heart talk. Shannon wants to be an artist when she grows up.

Erin is our second child, another daughter. She is eleven years old. She is very charming, having been gifted with all the "blarney" she could squeak out of the Irish part of her heritage. For the most part, so far, she is very even tempered. She fits the profile of the "second child" very well. It doesn't bother her to have not had all the "firsts" though she wishes she were an only child. Erin's favorite time is when all the other kids have something to do, or at their friend's houses and she gets to be alone with mommy and daddy. Of course, she hasn't hit the teenage years yet. When she does, Shannon will not be quite through with them yet, so I am dreading this stage. With all the split personalities that come along with the teenage years I fear I will be living with Sybil times two.

Erin has a lot of self-confidence. Maybe a little too much. She and her sister do not get along. They cannot agree on the color of the sky or the time of day. They are at the ages where, no matter what the other one says, she is wrong. Compliments are as rare as earthquakes, and neither one of them can find their way to the kitchen sink with their dirty dishes. They fight like cats and dogs, or more to the point, tigers and pit bulls. It is constant and it is getting on my nerves.

Shannon likes to pick on Erin until she cries. Erin will then throw something at Shannon and a brawl will break out, the likes of which the WWF could not hold a candle to. There is screaming, kicking, biting, pinching, hair pulling, name-calling and it does not stop until I am over them with a hairbrush. They know I have no intention of brushing their hair with it. They calm down and tell me that it was absolutely the other one's fault, "She started it!" "No I didn't, you started it!" The only thing stopping this fight from beginning all over again is the raised hairbrush. I tell my girls that my sisters and I used to fight like this and now, I cannot go one single day without talking to both of them. They are my best friends. The girls give me a look and tell me to get dressed. They are taking me to a nursing home, as my Alzheimer's is now out of control and they can't deal with it.

Erin is more athletic. Shannon is more artistic. Where Shannon wants to work for Walt Disney, Erin's life's ambition for the longest time was to be a waitress on roller skates. This year she wants to be a teacher. Neither one of the girls is very academic. I am not saying that they are not smart. They just choose not to

7

apply themselves any more than they have to. After all, if they waste all their energy on learning, how could they possibly have yet another battle when they walk in the door from school. It is exhausting.

This brings us to Robby, our third child and first son. He is eight years old. I never had a brother. My dad was the only male in our house. So when Robby was born, I just looked at my husband and told him, "This one is yours. I don't know what to do with it." I learned very quickly. Being the only boy, his sisters spoiled him rotten. I wasn't allowed to scold him, even if he was sticking his fingers in a wall socket. "Mom, he's just a baby, leave him alone." At least the girls had something else to concentrate their energy on.

Robby is our middle child and he fits the role perfectly. He is a straight A student. He gets very upset if he brings home anything less on his papers. He loves to play baseball. He loves Pokemon$_{TM}$. I don't think little boys in this age group are allowed to live in this country if they don't love Pokemon$_{TM}$. He looks exactly like his father. He must if my father was willing to admit that he didn't look as Irish as our side of the family. He is at the age where every parent loves his or her children to be. He is too afraid to talk back much, yet not afraid to show his emotions.

Robby tries to act like a big boy. He won't cry unless he is home. He has, however, inherited along with his father's good looks, his father's German temper. He likes to win. He likes to get his own way. When he doesn't, he pouts. He could teach a class on pouting he is so good at it. He then stomps out of the room. He could teach a class on stomping as well. But he never talks back. He will do anything I ask him to, the first time I ask him to. With the girls, the hair could grow on my legs to the point of needing to be shaved again, before they even get off the couch. He views his good behavior as a stepping stone, a means to an end. We will be in the store and he will ask for something. I say "no" and then I am immediately reminded of how he always does everything he is told. I give in, Shannon and Erin start fighting again, and he is happy.

He wants to be a professional baseball player when he grows up. I tell him that he can be anything he wants to be, as long as he is willing to work hard for it. He pouts, stomps his feet and walks out of the room.

This brings us to Casey, our fourth child and third daughter. She is six years old. When she was born, Robby was immediately proclaimed "The King" in our house. Casey is very petite. She is also very whiney. As a matter of fact, I am trying to get her a job whining the National Anthem at baseball games. We might as well put her talents to good use. She has made the word "mommy" into a five-syllable word, as in "mo-om-mm-me-ee". She is my "clingy" child. She prefers to drape herself over me twenty-four hours a day. She hangs on me all of the time.

Casey is the "snitch" in our house. The other kids can't wipe their noses without Casey telling on them. She has taken it upon herself to inform me of their every movement all day long. It has gotten to the point where I have told her unless the police are at the door, or there is a limb in a place it should not be, I don't want to hear about it. I don't care, let Shannon and Erin kill each other. The house would be quieter. Casey then whines that I don't care about her and what she has to say. When this one reaches the teenage years I am going to invest in a good set of earplugs. I can't even imagine how the teenager insults sound in a perfect pitch whine. Between Casey's whine and Shannon's teenage years, I can only surmise a teenager must whine twenty times louder and longer than a six year old.

Casey is also a very good student, or at least seems to be from what we can tell from kindergarten. She is the youngest girl of my parents' ten grandchildren. She loves this position. One of my sisters has two girls, the youngest of which is 14, so she longs to have the "little girl" days back. My other sister has three boys, so she just likes playing with girls. Hence, Casey is the one everyone wants to fawn over. My nieces will have her over and dress her up. They will play Barbies$_{TM}$ and house with her. I think all girls miss these activities when they grow out of them, so they find little girls to pretend they have to play with this stuff. Even Shannon and Erin will play with Casey, though not at the same time. Casey is the baby girl of our family and she is milking that status for all it is worth.

TJ is our fifth child, and youngest son. He is four years old. His real name is Thomas Joseph, though we believe the T should stand for "Terminator". He is single-handedly trying to level my house, destroy my sanity, and give his dad a stroke from causing him to scream his blood pressure into the danger range. For the most part, he is succeeding. TJ is as cute as a button, but a big boy for his age. At age four, he weighs 60 pounds and wears a size 8. Casey does not like this. Most people think he is older than her, being as I cannot get her out of a size 4T. She is however, insulted by this. Can people not see her maturity far outweighs his size? Well, if they can't, she will just whine about it. After all, TJ is still wearing diapers. Yes, at four years old, I cannot get this child potty trained. But there is whole chapter coming up on that. I couldn't cover that subject with just one sentence.

TJ has a goal in life. In fact, he has several. They all have to do with making me crazy. He intends to make sure that not one inch of carpet in our house is without a stain, no CD will play more than once before being snapped in half, and no toy will last more than 24 hours. He also wants to empty every nail polish bottle on the planet onto some piece of furniture in our house. He is currently experimenting on the capacity of a VCR to hold a peanut butter sandwich. This little experiment alone is breaking us in VCR purchases. TJ is a powerhouse. He is adorable. He has blond hair and big blue eyes, and he can melt me with his big smiles and hugs. I am also pretty sure he is responsible for at least half of my gray hair. The teenager gets the credit for much of the rest of it. He scares me with most of the things he does and infuriates me with the rest of the things he does. But when he goes to bed at night, he tells me I am the best mommy in the world and he loves me. Then he asks me to sing him a lullaby. He sucks his thumb and goes to sleep.

Who could ask for anything more?

3
ℰMy Gray Hair

Having introduced you to my children, I can now explain how they have strategically placed each gray hair on my head. I used to say that I was going to glide into my middle age with grace and dignity. I was not going to dye my hair. A little gray showed strength and character didn't it? Who cares if you have a few gray hairs after 40? I have since changed my mind. I have even told my children that if I die in between dye jobs, they are to get a magic marker as close to the color of my hair as possible and color in the gray so I look good in the casket. How pathetic is that? Well, they can do that for me in the end. After all, are they not the reason my hair was gray in the first place?

My father used to say that he could tell us where each gray hair on his head came from, implying that it was all from worrying about us. My sisters and I hold nothing on my brood. We were good girls. My older sister never even tried smoking. My younger sister and I did, but apart from that we were a piece of cake. At least I think we were. I could write a second book on my gray hair syndrome and the events that led up to it.

There is the whole process of giving birth. If that is not enough to make one look like the bride of Frankenstein, I don't know what is. However, as most parents are keenly aware, birthing the child is the easiest part of the whole process. Once the child is born you have to raise it. You have to give your child

12

insight and wisdom, when they don't even want to hear your first name. I think three of my kids would be hard pressed to tell you my first name.

I am pretty sure St. Michael is upstairs right now putting check marks next to my name for all the things I am doing wrong as a mother and I am beginning to think there is a correlation between this and my gray hair. Gray hairs are like the little check marks of bad parenting. It seems like every time I screw up, a gray hair pops up. Believe me, no one is worse at good parenting than me. You would think by the time I had the fifth kid I would have some idea of what to do with them. But they are all so different. I believe our family gene pool is akin to the Atlantic Ocean. How could five kids from the same two parents behave so differently?

Shannon of course, at 13, is responsible for the latest crop of gray hair. She has decided that I am her friend, not her mother. She tried to call me "Nan", but after the lecture she had to endure about how I deserved respect from her after raising her with all the sweat and blood my body could muster, she decided, for the time being, she would continue to call me "mom". I don't even want to know how she refers to me with her friends.

Of course, as any parent of a teenager learns, the teenager knows everything. We know nothing. We taught them all the things they know but we are stupid. The day Shannon turned 13, I, of course, turned into a moron, complete with the inability to see that she had piled on make-up and was wearing a shirt three sizes too small for her. She awoke on her thirteenth birthday, went into the bathroom, and came out looking as if she was ready to turn her first trick. I gasped. She looked at me as if the moron transition had been completed. "What is on your face?" I asked. "Make up," she replied, implying, "you moron." "It looks more like poster paint," I say shyly, realizing that she thinks my brain is the size of a raisin. Then, in that tone that only a teenager has perfected, she regales, "Well, you said I could wear make up when I turned thirteen and today I am thirteen and I am going to wear make up because I think I look great!" "If you wear that make up to school, there is a good chance we will both get arrested. Now you have a choice. Either you go back in the bathroom and wash that off, or I am going to get your father's sander and start chipping away at it. What's it going to be?" As she stumbles back into the bathroom, I can hear her mumbling, "You are such a liar. You make promises that you don't keep. You said I could wear make up when I was thirteen and now you are making me take it off. I hate school. I hate this house. I hate my life. . ." I can feel the gray hair sprouting literally, out the top of my head. What did the harlot I just encountered do with my daughter? Yesterday, when she was still twelve, she knew her boundaries. Today, because she turned thirteen, she is a shrew. It was as if being thirteen gave her all the answers, as if some rite of passage had been given to her. Well, being a teenager does come with a rite of passage, but along with it comes responsibility, which Shannon has yet to learn. Let's just say I sprouted a new crop of gray hair that day, covered very nicely by red blonde #10 thank you.

14

Erin gave me her share of my grayness at a young age. She did eat, however you would not believe the things this child would put in her mouth. I used to think if they pumped her stomach I would be immediately arrested for feeding her things that were not food. Poison Control and I were on a first name basis for a while when Erin was younger. She liked to eat things that were not in the "food" category. She liked to eat soap. This didn't bother me too much. I knew it wouldn't hurt her. Poison Control told me it wouldn't. In fact, it kept her quite regular. When she was thirteen months old, Erin and my nephew got into the bathroom and chewed off the childproof cap on a bottle of children's Tylenol®, the grape flavored ones. Of course they ate them. Poison Control told me to give them ipecac, the stuff that makes them throw up. You do not want to hear the details. Suffice to say that it is possible to hold two vomiting babies at one time, and not get any on the bathroom floor, if your toilet and bathtub are in close enough proximity. I proved it.

Erin then decided she liked deodorant, not under her arms, in her mouth. She ate an entire bar of it. My friends at Poison Control assured me that she was okay; just give her lots of water. Her next snack consisted of an inkpad that was once blue. By the time I found her with it only her mouth was blue. The inkpad was white. She had sucked the ink out of the inkpad. I must say I panicked a little on this one, but you gotta love Poison Control. They once again, confirmed that this too, was nontoxic. Shannon had a doll set with little silverware and you guessed it, Erin ate a knife, fork and spoon. I didn't know this of course, until the complete set came out in her diaper the next day. Erin now swims competitively. I can't help but wonder if she really enjoys it, or is she trying to drink an entire pool to wash down all the non-food things she ate as a baby. I will keep wondering, and more gray hair will pop up.

Robby, my eight-year-old son, has had a calmer childhood. Generally, he is more docile than the girls. Of course there was the time he hurled himself out of the crib, onto the floor, and broke his collarbone. I called the doctor as my pediatrician was away on vacation. The covering doctor would not see him, and told me that even if his collarbone was broken, there was nothing they would do. He would be fine. He was just over a year old and would not lift his arm. I did not see this as fine. We waited until our pediatrician was back and he confirmed that Robby did, indeed, have a broken collarbone. Can you see the gray hair?

Casey, my six-year-old daughter, is just trying to whine a few more gray hairs out of me. She is developing what I call the "Jezebel effect". She is beginning to like make-up at the age of six. This is because her sisters use her as their "model" for new make-up. "Let's try this out on Casey. She'll think we are playing with her." The next thing I know Casey looks like she is getting ready for Halloween, when it is only June. Then she begins to whine that the girls are making her do stuff and she whines that she is hungry and she whines that she doesn't want to play any-more . . . like I said, she is whining gray hair out of me.

TJ, my four-year-old son, makes the gray hair come out in droves. His very presence is like fertilizer on my gray hair grassy knoll. TJ gets within ten feet of me and the hair just turns gray. I think my hair realizes if it just turns gray, then maybe he won't do whatever he was going to do to make it turn gray, and thus, the planet will be safe for another few minutes. Just the other day, TJ decided to help daddy make French fries. For his part, he was going to get the Fry Daddy®, full of oil. His plan went awry and two quarts of oil got spilled on my dining room carpet. I was seriously afraid of attracting rats, or maybe the police, as my husband was screaming so loud you could hear him out on the highway. He was banging his fists on the dining room table as if that was going to make TJ come out from under it. TJ survived, Bob calmed down, and my gray hair became so prominent from that episode that I immediately called my stylist for an appointment.

4
ᗣ Where Are My Keys

Everyone at some time or another has lost something and cannot remember where they left it. This happens to me quite often, maybe daily. I lose pens a lot. I can never find one when I need one. I have come up with a theory. There are a lot of saints up in Heaven. They must be very busy people. I think if they need a pen and cannot find one, they just reach down out of the clouds and take mine. It is the perfect crime. I look for that pen for days, swearing that I left in exactly the same spot. St. Ignatius will then return my pen. It will turn up in that exact same spot and I will just believe my insanity is deepening. I know I looked there and it was NOT there before. Of course it wasn't. St. Ignatius was signing his new car lease.

Another theory I have is that everything on this earth can grow legs and walk when nobody is looking. I am pretty sure everything in my house walks around all night long because when I get up in the morning, nothing seems to be where it was before, let alone where I left it before going to bed.

If my husband loses something, it is my fault. If the kids lose something, it is my fault. I do not like the fact that the mom inherits the blame for losing everything. If I ask the children where was the last time they saw their item, let's say it is a shirt, they become idiots, total idiots. They have no idea what I am talking about. They don't even remember owning a shirt. See, even their memories grow legs and walk off. However, when I find the shirt, their memories suddenly fly back into their heads and they each claim the shirt as theirs. This shirt, which fifteen seconds ago no one had any idea what I was talking about, is suddenly the only one each of him or her had and they are sure it is theirs because it has some mark on it. When I remind them that no one knew what I was talking about when I first asked where it was then tell me, "We didn't know you were talking about that shirt. It is MINE!"

The most classic lost item would be the car keys. I think my car keys have more than two legs because they are lost all of the time. Even if I had a set of car keys with a beeper to find them if I lost them, I would lose the beeper. You see the only time I do lose my car keys is when I am in a hurry. If I have three days to get somewhere, my keys sit on my lap like a puppy waiting to be petted. However, when I am late for an appointment with my boss, those same dependable keys are now playing a very immature game of hide and seek. Their legs are moving in overdrive as they go from hiding space to hiding space, wanting me to lose my job so I can sit with them on my lap some more.

I lost my youngest son, TJ, in the mall once. For a second I considered slipping out of the mall, as no one else had noticed I lost a child. I was not showing that look of panic that moms of only one child show when Johnny strolls away for a second. I figured if I left TJ at the mall I could go home and get some work done. He would eventually tell somebody it was my fault he walked away from me and the police would come knocking with him in tow. I just calmly went to the pet store. My kids always drift off to the pet store when we are at the mall. There he was, crying for a guinea pig.

I do miss my mind, though. It grew its legs a little over four years ago when I had my last child and it has hidden itself very well. Maybe St. Ignatius needed my mind for a few years. Right around the birth of our last child is the last time I can remember putting a single tangible thought together. Time since then has been a blur of feedings, diaper changing, refereeing fights, watching mindless television, washing clothes, making lunches, screaming, yelling, begging, and pleading each day until I fall into bed exhausted at the end of the day. Maybe when the kids are all grown and out of the house, my mind won't be so afraid anymore, and it will come out of hiding and jump back into my head. Until then, I guess I will have to settle for being happy in my insanity.

5
Potty Training

To anyone who has ever potty trained or tried to potty train a toddler, my hat's off to you. I would rather go through childbirth 37 more times then potty train one more toddler. At least with childbirth, you get some good drugs that help ease the experience. With potty training, you are on your own. I have potty trained four children before this, and with my youngest, TJ, I am truly a failure. He is four and a half and has no intention of ever using the potty. He just doesn't care. I am beginning to think I shouldn't either.

Shannon, my oldest, got potty trained by virtue of the chicken pox. The pox were all over her butt. I convinced her that if she were wearing panties instead of diapers, the pox wouldn't itch as much. She was three and a half. It seemed pretty easy at that time. Erin was a little tougher. By the time her potty training experience began, Robby had already been born and Erin already had the chicken pox. I had to use another method. I tried the "You're the big sister" routine and told her that she had to show the baby that she could use the potty. She needed to show him she was a "big girl". Somehow, it worked. She was also three and a half when she learned to use the potty.

When it came time to train Robby, I was at a loss. Personally, I had never had a brother and had never seen my dad naked. I was clueless. I told Bob it was his job to potty train Robby. Of course, it was easy for Bob. He took Robby into the bathroom and told him he could stand up and go to the potty. They played crossfire with their streams. Robby loved it. He went to the bathroom about twenty seven times a day, just to be a "big boy". Of course, Bob neglected to tell him there were certain times when he had to sit down to go the potty. After scrubbing the bathroom floor a few times from "accidents" Robby was trained, and I didn't have to do it. He was also three and a half and I was beginning to think this was the magic age, every child in the world would potty train at three and a half years old.

Casey somehow got potty trained. I am really not sure how, as she was only eighteen months old when TJ was born and all the time after that is pretty much a blur. For all I know, some stranger could have come in and trained her, or maybe she just got sick of being ignored because the baby was here. It doesn't matter. She wears underwear now so at some point she started using the potty.

TJ however, has no intention of ever using the potty. He is four and a half, wears size 8 clothes and diapers. He is getting ready to go to preschool and I need to have him trained. He wears the largest diapers available so if he doesn't get the hang of it soon, I am going to have to start buying Depends. I think he knows how to use the potty, he just doesn't want to. It is easier for ME to do all the work.

He will tell me when he needs to be changed. "Mommy, change my diaper" he says. "If you're so smart, go change your own diaper" I tell him. "No, you have to change me," he continues, "or I will get a sore hiney." The child knows he will get a sore hiney if he sits in poop, but he will NOT use that damn potty. I've tried the potty chair. He peed all over it. I don't think he will ever have a career in archery. His aim is terrible. I even tried just putting him in pants and letting him feel the wet. Maybe he wouldn't like it and start using the potty. Well, after we replaced most of the furniture and had the rugs cleaned until they are threadbare, I abandoned this idea.

I asked my pediatrician. He asked TJ if he was afraid of the potty. TJ asked him what his stethoscope was. He doesn't care what the doctor thinks, either. I tried putting him on the potty every half hour. Every once in a while he would squeeze out a turd the size of a pea and expect me to dance around as if he had just won the Nobel Prize. I would, and five minutes later he would come to me walking as if he just got off a horse with a diaper full. I guess he didn't like my dance.

I know his mission in life is to have me committed before he starts school or at least before he ever goes on a potty. I know we are in an age where we aren't supposed to force our children to do anything. They are to be their own person and do things in their own time. Well then, I think we are going to have to change our college applications a little bit. One of the questions will need to be, "Are you potty trained?" This way they can put roommates together with the same problem. TJ will need to find one of those roommates.

6
Show and Tell

I have five children, as I have said before. Their schools do a lot of things that annoy me, such as homework on weekends (I don't have the time). However, there is none so annoying a thing as kindergarten "Show and Tell". This is a barbaric practice that dates back to the cave days when the small cave children would bring their latest kill into school and show the cave teacher. All the children would ooh and ahh and then they would all eat the thing right down to the carcass, which they would then whittle into little Pebbles-like hair bones. At that time it was probably a great idea, being as they did not have say, textbooks and blackboards, and the cave moms did not have anything better to do then help their little cave children drag their kill to the cave school.

"Show and Tell" has evolved over the years. During "Show and Tell" when I was in kindergarten (not too long after the cave days, according to my children), we just brought in any toy we had laying around and showed it to the class. Then we went back to finger-painting and playing store. There was very little learning in kindergarten in my day, but a lot of playtime.

However, today, the children have to LEARN in kindergarten. Our children are not allowed to play store until they can count all the items in the store and tell what letter each one begins with. Hence, "Show and Tell" has become the biggest nuisance since easy open packaging. Now "Show and Tell" must be part of the learning experience. In my children's school, you have a letter of the week. The "Show and Tell" must begin with that letter. The "Show and Tell" must then be put in a large paper bag with three clues written on it. The other children in the class have to guess what you brought in for "Show and Tell", all the while remembering that it has to start with the letter of the week. I am thinking Vanna White had something to do with this. She was probably starting to worry that her job might be obsolete if she didn't make the world "letter obsessive-compulsive".

Anyway, I always forget which day my daughter has "Show and Tell". I also forget which day she has gym, which day she has library (my family has solely funded the library in fines), and four out of five days I forget to make her lunch. I told you I am not bucking for Mother of the Year. I am just hoping to come out of this whole parenting thing alive.

Casey and Robby are all bundled up and ready to walk out the door to get the bus when Casey turns around and yells those six little words that make my blood run cold, "I HAVE SHOW AND TELL TODAY!" I would rather hear Turkey Lurkey tell me the sky is falling. She then informs that the letter of the week is V or G. Thank you, Mrs. Z. The letter of the week couldn't be D, as we have enough dolls to fill a landfill. It also couldn't be T, as we have enough trucks to fill the landfill next the doll landfill. No, we have to get V and G, and I am furiously trying to think of something, ANYTHING, that begins with either one of these letters. The only things that come to mind are Vodka and Gin, both of which I could put my hands on, and both of which start with the proper "letter", but I am thinking this is probably not a good idea, glass bottles and all.

I am frantically searching through the four toy boxes we have in the house, of which three have been emptied onto various floors in the rooms in which they are housed. I finally find a Godzilla. I was never so happy to see this monster toy, whose sole purpose in life up to this point was to make impressions on the bottoms of my feet when I stepped on it on my way to the bathroom at 3:00 a.m. My daughter, in tears, informs me that Godzilla is a boys' toy and besides, this particular Godzilla is missing an arm. For a moment I wonder if the arm is imbedded in my foot. Being the fast thinker that I am, I inform her that this makes him Gimpy Godzilla, a double G word, which would probably get her extra credit. She cries louder.

Okay, back to the search. We have 37,000 Hot Wheels® in one of these toy boxes and I could not, for the life of me, put my hands on a bleeping van if you begged me. I am now making up names for ambiguous looking toys, seeing which one will catch her fancy and stop her from screaming. She didn't know what a "vixen" was, so Barbie™ had to stay Barbie™. I told her we could shove daddy in a bag and she could take him to school as a "grouch". This did not float either.

Finally, at the bottom of toy box number four, dust covered and with one hand chewed, I see it - GUMBY™!!! Voila! Every kindergarten kid knows Gumby™! We shove Gumby™ in the shopping bag, write down his three clues, which to all Gumby™

26

fans everywhere, are obvious: *1.* He's green.   *2.* He's clay.
3. He has a pony friend.

Another crisis averted, except for the fact that Casey's four-year-old brother, TJ, is now screaming at the top of his lungs that this was HIS Gumby$_{TM}$, and he was going to play with him all day, and she can't take him to school, and nobody loves him . . .

I can't wait for S day. I am going to send in my straight jacket and she can show all the kindergarten children how Casey's mommy spends her days.

7

ℰ The Radiation Monster
Better Known As The Television

In a perfect world, according to my children, every house would have a television in every room, wide screen, cable ready, and Play Station® attached. Wouldn't all the problems of the world be solved by this single solution? Well, you could look at it this way. We wouldn't have to worry about where the kids were at any given time, we would know. They would be in front of their own television either playing Tomb Raider XII or just watching the Game Show Network. What an intelligent class of human beings we would be raising.

The television and the arguments that go along with it are responsible for my terrible disposition most of the time and my husband's gastric problems. I am jealous of this monster. My children love it more than they love me. They listen to it better than they listen to me. They actually worship it. And of course, they fight over it. In the middle of a TV argument I will announce, "I am going to the store, anybody want to come?" They look at me as if to say, "How could you possibly even suggest that we leave our first love to go somewhere with you?" They make that face that looks as if they just tasted liver for the first time. Then they go back to mutilating each other.

The little guys, of course, have not had enough Barney yet. They are only up to three hours a day, and I think, in order to stay a true Barney supporter, you have to be able to quote Barney and Baby Bop from each show of the day, which takes at least a good five hours of Barney. They are crying that they can't hear Baby Bop's new song. NEW???? There hasn't been a new Barney episode in three years!!!!! They must know this one by heart!!!!!!

Robby, at age eight, has no sympathy. He is just over the Barney phase and totally into baseball. You have to be if your life's ambition is to pitch for the Phillies. To him, it is not an ambition, it is a fact. He just needs to get a little older before he will allow the Phillies to recruit him. Of course, to that end, he is in desperate need to watch twenty hours a day of baseball. I tried to tell him that in order to pitch for the Phillies, he needs to actually go outside and throw a ball around but he seems to be convinced this skill will osmose through the television to him. Again, the monster rules. He is screaming at the little guys that Barney is "gay" and he is too old to watch Barney. Don't they see his need to watch baseball all the time is much more important? He tells me in no uncertain terms, that the television is his for the next two hours.

Shannon and Erin, of course, are in need of an MTV fix. I hate this channel. I am convinced it is the modern day equivalent of the Vulcan Mind Meld from Star Trek. MTV has kids all over the country glued to it. I guess I would have loved this channel twenty or so years ago. Back then we only had three channels on the television and our parents were the sole possessors. We could watch Bewitched and the Brady Bunch, if, and only if, our homework was done, we had our baths and our teeth were brushed. I tell my kids how my parents would have never allowed us to watch this much television and guess what? They rolled their eyes at me. I remember my father telling me once that if I rolled my eyes at him one more time, he knew exactly where, on the back of my head, he could hit me real hard and my eyes would roll right OUT of my head. It scared me to death and I never rolled my eyes at him again. I told my kids this and they burst out laughing. It became a game with them, each trying to decide where they would keep their eyes after I shot them out of their heads. Well, at least it was enough of a diversion for my husband to sneak in and put the History Channel on. And you know they don't even think about talking back to him. I think he practices the Vulcan Mind Meld. I haven't perfected it quite yet.

8
Bedtime For Hansteins

How many times in your life have you said, "If I had only known that when I was younger"? "Oh to know what I know now and be twenty years younger" or something like that. Anyway, bedtime is one of those things. No child ever wants to go to bed, ever! If someone told me at 7:30 at night that I had to go to bed, I would leave skid marks I would be running so fast to get under those warm covers and not have to do dishes, wash the next day's clothes or go over homework for the ninetieth time. I would be asleep before anybody could come looking for me and I would not, under any circumstances, get out of that bed before the next morning. I would take full advantage of 11 to 12 hours of sleep.

Alas, as I have said before, there is a conspiracy out to get me. I think you are starting to see the pattern. Not one of my children feels the same way I do about bedtime. My husband agrees with me, but he is usually asleep on the couch before dinner is served, so his vote doesn't count. I usually start at dinner time, telling the kids they better make sure their homework is done, get their clothes ready for tomorrow, get their baths and go to bed. Sounds quite simple and so routine, doesn't it? You see, I really could be routine if only the troops would cooperate. I think I have enough kids to constitute a platoon so I think I should be allowed to carry out the same punishments: dishonorable discharge, shackles, solitary confinement, etc. However, until the law sees things the way I do, I have to settle for just yelling, complaining and trying to make them cooperate.

After dinner the first thing the children do is gravitate towards the television. I considered having a television embedded in my abdomen so I could get them to follow me, but I was a little worried about the times that one of them absolutely has to watch a show when someone else is watching something else. I would be forced to stand against a wall on one foot in order to get the perfect reception so that they can watch yet another "Cartoon Network" rerun. This did not appeal to me.

For the next hour after dinner I will continually remind them that they have only half an hour before bedtime, so they better have their clothes laid out and their teeth brushed, showers done, etc. That and fifty cents will get you a phone call, as they all swear to me they are ready for the next day. It is now about 9:00 p.m. and even the little guys are still not in bed. Bob, my husband, is snoring on the couch and occasionally rouses himself to yell in a grumbled voice, "Do as your mother tells you". Well, that certainly has them shaking in their slippers. A man who can't even focus his gaze is certainly no threat to their television watching. They continue to stare at the cable ready monster.

By about 10:00 p.m., I have had it. This occurs to me every night around this time and they know it. At least I am consistent with something. My alter ego, the Banshee, takes over and I go into the living room and slam the off button on the television.

They all look at me as if I have just transformed into the Incredible Hulk. I am shaking uncontrollably and my face is beet red as I scream, "GO TO BBBBEEEEEDDDDDD!!!!!!!" Then, these children have the audacity to look scared. I have only been screaming for two hours now that they need to go to bed. They scramble like cockroaches with a flashlight just turned on them. There are kids running in every direction. This is pretty funny since the bedrooms are all in the same direction. Like a scene out of Sleepy Hollow, I begin to chase them to their rooms. As I have said before, look up dysfunction in the dictionary and there our family portrait will be.

Of course, this all calms down for about ten minutes. Then, the whispering begins. These children, who cannot get As in English or Social Studies, could whisper the Gettysburg Address as long as it means they do not have to go to sleep. The two oldest girls have to start picking on each other. Shannon starts on Erin, Erin answers back. This argument starts out as a whisper and ends up with me standing at their doorway; unable to speak I am so angry. The Banshee is back. Now, correct me if I am wrong, but if I saw an actual banshee standing in my doorway, I would shut up! You would not hear another word out of my mouth. However my girls know that if they stop talking they will actually fall asleep and what good would that do on their quest to have me committed? They look at me with a "pretend to be scared" look and I go back to bed. After about 35 reminders of "Go to sleep girls", "You're grounded for a month, girls", "I will cancel the cable, girls" they finally go to sleep.

Just when I thought it was safe to go to sleep and continue my ongoing affair with Richard Gere, my kindergartner, Casey, says in her smallest tired whine, "I need a poster board for tomorrow, mommy. Good night, I love you!" The Banshee has been defeated once again.

9
⌒Now The Hansteins Need To Wake Up

Of course after a rousing nighttime game of "Let's try to get mommy committed", the children are too tired to get up in the morning for school. This comes as no surprise to me. I only told them this sixty five times the night before. I start my day at about 6:00 a.m. Now, by my calculations, the children have now only had about six hours of sleep, compared to most children's ten to twelve hours of sleep. These are the children of the anal retentive parents. My kids are much more fun even if they are grumpy and tired.

I get up and wake my husband, who by now has had the required amount of sleep for a bear in hibernation. He does not get up. He needs a few more minutes. I then wake the two oldest girls as they have to get the first bus. After about a dozen attempts to be nice, the Banshee returns. She has not had enough sleep either, so now she is a cranky, tired banshee. "Get out of that bed, or I will bulldoze the house and you will be swallowed up in a pile of rubble and I am NOT going to tell you again." This usually gets them moving with comments like, "What's wrong with you?" as they stumble towards the bathroom.

I begin to gingerly wake the next two children who have to get their bus in about thirty minutes. The whiner wakes up whining, "I can't go to school today. I will miss you too much." "What you will be missing," I begin, "is a room full of toys if you do not get up, brush your teeth and get dressed . . . and stop whining." My son, Robby, gets up and stomps around because he is tired. I really have to wonder how many times you tell a child he will be tired in the morning if he does not get to bed on time before it sinks in. I am up to about 35,000 times and it has not yet registered. Maybe I should buy some subliminal tapes and play them to the children during prime time television, as this is the only time they seem to have any concentration.

Of course the youngest is up. The younger you are, the less sleep you require. The youngest is always up first. However, during the frenzy to get the bus on time, he feels that I should stop what I am doing; which is making lunches, combing hair, packing back packs, signing permission slips, going over last minute test questions, and make him a six course breakfast. Since I will not stop my morning ritual to do this, he will just lay on the floor and scream. What he does not realize is that by the time I'd given birth to child number five, lying on the floor and screaming does not bother me. With the first child, I ran every time she sighed. By the time the fifth child came along well, let me say he has to be pretty much not breathing before I can muster up the strength to take care of whatever it is he needs.

It is time for my husband to get up and he now commands the bathroom, of which we have only one, for a shower. The girls are furious. They have only gotten to empty one bottle of hairspray on their heads this morning, and therefore their matted hair will be flopping in the wind every time they move. Somehow, though, my husband says, "I'm going to take a shower" and they scatter like the wind. Maybe I am using the wrong words. Every time they don't listen, I have decided I am going to yell, "I'm going to take a shower!" and see what happens. For some reason, however, when my husband says it, it means that they cannot go within a one-mile radius of the bathroom until he is finished. When I say it, it is an open invitation to come tell me all of life burdens, ask me what they can have for a snack, tell on their brother or sister, explain why they failed a test ("The teacher hates me"), beg for a few bucks to go to the Mall or just come sit on the toilet so that I am not lonely in the shower.

With much screaming, cajoling, promising Slurpees®, begging, threatening to take away the television if they miss the bus, the children finally make the bus. I am now ready for a good day's sleep. However, the screamer is still at it. I give up for the first time that day. "Get your coat," I say, "We're going to McDonalds®." He stops screaming.

10
I Hate Traffic

Some people love to drive. My husband loves to drive. We drove to Florida with five children under the age of 9 he loves to drive so much. I hate to drive. I am the most paranoid driver in the world. I think every driver, in every car, is out to get me, and I am beginning to realize, for the most part, this is absolutely true.

For example, I start out my morning late, as usual, and I have to get the kids to school. Two different schools on this particularly late morning. The kids throw some cereal down and gulp a glass of milk. I pile them into the car and off we go. I pull out onto the main road and I am cruising along. I can see the car waiting at the next crossroad. He has plenty of time to pull out but seems to be waiting for an engraved invitation or a message from God because he just sits there. As I get closer, I realize he now does not have enough time to pull out in front of me, or so I thought. He now becomes Richard Petty as he breaks the sound barrier to squeal his car out in front of me. "Damn!" I am thinking, he must be really late for, like, his wedding or something.

Now that he has established his place in front of me, I am thinking I will get the kids to school on time. I will just cruise along behind this accomplished speedster. He then gazes in his rearview mirror and sees that it is I behind the wheel of that minivan. He immediately coasts to a cool seven miles per hour and begins to sightsee, which in our neighborhood could take a long time. It could be a while before anything worth looking at catches his eye. Now, why in the hell did that guy make getting out onto the street in front of me his top priority thirty seconds ago, and now his top priority is to see that my children are illiterate, because at this rate, they are going to miss the entire school year? I could get them to school faster if we happened to see a turtle towing a houseboat and hitched a ride. He did it because he saw ME in the rearview mirror. I am not paranoid.

The traffic lights must have eyes too. Either that or the idiot who times those stupid things never passed the word problem section of his elementary school math class. For example, how long will it take a car to get to the next traffic light after the current traffic light turns green? This would be the precise time to allow the next light to turn green. In reality, you have just enough time to speed up so that you can leave half your tire tread behind trying to stop when you get to that next light as it turns yellow and then immediately red. Of course, when you regain consciousness after hitting your head on the steering wheel, it will be green again.

Red, yellow, green, arrows, right turn on red, why don't they just take away all the traffic lights, stop and yield signs and let us fend for ourselves? I think we could do a better job just winging it. We might bang into each other once in a while, but my husband works in auto body repair. It will keep him busy and out of my hair.

11
⌒Reserved Parking Spaces

It's early afternoon on a Tuesday and I decide to go grocery shopping. This is an activity that I enjoy as a mother of a large family and I always make sure I have a lot of time to devote to it. However, that usually means that I have to go to the grocery store with at least two of the five children in tow. This does not make my day.

However, as is customary in my life, my day can always get worse. This is the motto that I live by. That in mind, I pack up the two youngest children and head to the grocery store. I am in the frame of mind that I can handle the kids as long as I open the first bag of candy I see. That is, if I can get that far.

I pull into the parking lot, and I am beginning to think that the grocery store has been blessed by a visit from the President of the United States. There is not one single parking space, that is of course, except for the 24 empty handicapped spots across the very front of the grocery store. Now, I have no problem with preferred parking for the handicapped people. It is absolutely necessary and people with handicaps should not have to tackle a half-mile walk into the store. I have a little trouble, however, believing that 40 or so handicapped people would all decide to go to the grocery store at exactly the same time, unless of course there is an underground handicapped railroad that tells all handicapped people when they can go to the grocery store. I really don't think this is the case, as I have never seen every one of these parking spaces taken in one given trip to the grocery store.

There are people parking half a mile away to buy $300.00 worth of groceries, most of which will melt by the time they make it back to their car.

That is however, not the point of this chapter. It is the latest trend in the parking wars. Now we have extra spots for pregnant women. Where the hell were these parking spots when I could not see my own ankles? You know where? Three miles away, with the guy with the Rocky Road soup that used to be ice cream. I could never find a close parking space when I was in my ninth month and had to have asparagus with Fluff on it.

We also now have parking spaces "RESERVED FOR OUR SENIORS". This is a great idea, assuming that the seniors parking in these spaces deserve to be driving, but that is another issue altogether. Our senior citizens should be able to park closer than the younger people. We will all be short of breath and have muscle aches one day, probably sooner than we think.

We are, however, leaving out one important part of our culture that desperately need a close place to park. The parking sign would say something like "RESERVED FOR STRESSED OUT MOTHERS WITH UNRULY TODDLERS". If I have to park three miles away from the grocery store with my two youngest children with me, there is a good chance that I will go home with one less child than I arrived with. Anyone who decides to take two children under the age of five in any store puts their lives in their own hands anyway. All I have to do is turn the car off and these little guys are running as if they have been oxygen deprived for the two-minute drive to the grocery store. They bolt out of the car like potheads rolling out of a van at Woodstock.

Meanwhile, I am just getting out of the car and chasing a runaway cart down the main highway because I dislodged it as I tapped it with my bumper and I know if it causes an accident, I am going to be responsible for the damage. When I finally retrieve the runaway cart, I cannot find my children, who are playing hide and seek among the parked cars of the senior citizens who got the good spots next to the empty handicapped spots. A pregnant woman comes out to get into her car, parked in a premier spot and I look at her and say, "Just you wait. A year from now you will be next to me, chasing a cart and your child at the same time" and I add, "and guess what? There is no parking space for that!"

12
Martha Stewart

Let me start this chapter by saying that Martha Stewart, in spite of her current problems, is probably a very lovely lady. I have never met her. I don't want to meet her. If I ever do meet her, I am going to make her eat marshmallow cereal for dinner out of a Barbie bowl with a chip in it. If she survives that without having a massive coronary, I suppose we can be friends. She seems personable enough. I mean, she makes gobs of money telling people how easy it is to be elegant (I personally believe easy elegance is an oxymoron), makes her own paper, and has the cleanest, neatest house I have ever seen. Maybe you are starting to see where this friendship would go awry. She has real nerve. She really makes us moms who are just trying to stay afloat look really bad.

I have always said when I become filthy rich, as in when I hit the big lottery; I am going to buy the time slot on television after "Living" with Martha Stewart. My show will be called "Surviving After Watching Living - Life in the Real World". I mean, seriously, have you seen some of the things she does? She makes her own stationery, bakes cookies in three stages, and did you see the time she planted an entire garden for hardly any money? The last time I tried to create a garden, I spent a ridiculous amount of money. The squirrels and rabbits ate all the seeds and all I had to show for my effort was a big debit on my Visa® card and a yard full of manure. Some garden.

Of course there is the time she insisted we make lemon-curd meringue cookies for our weekend guests. I had her beat on this one. I went to the dollar store and bought some assorted "day olds" from the cookie department. My weekend guests, who usually consist of four or five kids from the neighborhood, went nuts. I was the best mom in the whole neighborhood. I let them eat cookies until they puked. If I had made lemon-curd meringue cookies, they would take one look at the lemon curd and someone would comment, "Ew, Mom, who hockered into your cookies?" It would just not be worth it. Maybe Martha has much more upscale weekend guests. I think President Bush would like chocolate chips every bit as much as Hocker Curd Meringue cookies. However, it wouldn't take me three hours and I wouldn't have to fluff my meringue. I would just roll up the package and throw it away, arrange the cookies on a nice tray and have a great visit with the Pres and the Mrs.

On another memorable episode, Martha was making her own paper. It was to be special personalized stationery. Most everyone knows when a note is arriving from me. It comes on a piece of paper ripped out of one of the kid's notebooks from school. Isn't that special? I don't have the time or the space to be making my own paper. My favorite store, the one where everything costs $1.00 has plenty of it, and at a good price. We have come a long way in this country just so that we DON'T have to make our own paper.

I do over twenty loads of laundry a week. I run the dishwasher

44

twice a day just to keep us in cereal bowls. I clock thousands of miles on my car with carpooling and grocery shopping. After a good soap opera and some Springer, what's left? I'll tell you what's left; a worn out mom who has just enough time to throw a meatloaf in the oven for dinner. I am not going to press my own paper, make lemon-curd meringue cookies, or put a garden in.

Martha Stewart should be ashamed of herself. My show will grab all of her ratings, as we will discuss whether or not Montel waxed his head enough for the last show, or how to keep the kids quiet during our favorite soap opera, etc. These are much more useful topics of discussion. My show would have 101 ways to shove everything you own into a closet if someone calls and says they are coming over, or how to disguise your dirty laundry pile so that it looks like an art exhibit, etc. Things people really need to know.

Our motto will be, "Kmart® is our savior". The funny thing is Kmart® has an entire line of Martha Stewart things like sheets and towels, all color and season coordinated. My followers will not be allowed to even look at those items. Anything that matches takes away from the aura of the artsy look of a cluttered home. We would all wear little buttons with Martha Stewart's picture on them with a big red line through it. Now that's living!

13
⟨My Certs® Addiction⟩

Everyone has to have a vice, right? For a while mine was Certs®. I think I had a serious addiction to Certs®. You know, the little lifesaver-like candies, with Retsyn and no hole. It was ridiculous. I had to have them with me all the time. I would buy them in bulk. I was even looking for a "Certs® Anonymous" program but I couldn't find one.

As with any addiction, mine started out small. I was in the grocery store and I thought I might like a breath mint so I picked up a pack of Certs®. It was a big mistake, but I didn't know that at the time. The next time I went to the grocery store, which was the next day (I go to the grocery store pretty much every day), I picked up two packs, one for the car and one for my purse. By the end of the week I was at the local wholesale club buying in bulk, 24 packs of Certs®. I figured they were low in calorie, though I don't think that counts if you eat four sleeves of them a day. I just couldn't get enough.

I realized I was in trouble when I started rolling my spare change for Certs® money, even when we needed milk. I was really glad Certs® were not illegal, as I would have been on a street corner trying to score some.

I decided to go cold turkey and just stop eating Certs®. This is akin to stopping heroin without the help of a methadone clinic. I was okay for about the first hour. I ate everything in the refrigerator, but I got by. After eating everything in the refrigerator, I cleaned the house. Then I made the kids clean their rooms. At least I was not eating Certs®. By the time the kids were done with their rooms, they were pleading, "Please mom, go have a Certs®. We can't take it anymore." "NO," I scream, "I am going to kick this habit if it kills me!" "It may kill us," their little voices pleaded. "Well at least I won't be eating Certs®!" I was so rational at this point.

I decided to try a support group but there is no support group for people who are addicted to little candies with Retsyn. I wondered what it would be like if I went to a Narcotics Anonymous meeting and told my story. Surely those people would understand. They knew what it was like to not want to go through another day without a fix. So what if the fix was candy and not drugs. Wasn't it sort of the same thing?

We would all be standing around drinking coffee. Then we would all take a seat and it would be someone's turn to speak. A guy would walk up to the microphone. He would say, "Hi my name is Joe and I am a heroin addict." "Hi Joe," everyone would reply. Joe would begin to unravel his story. He had lost his job, his wife and kids, even almost lost his life just to get his hands on heroin. Then he would tell us he had been clean for a year and he never felt better. We would all clap.

Then it would be my turn to get up. Boy would I feel stupid. What was I thinking? But I had an addiction. So I didn't lose my kids, but I didn't buy milk for them one night just to get another pack of Certs®. Wasn't that pretty awful? These people would understand. They would help me.

I would walk up to the microphone and say, "Hi my name is Nan and I have an addiction." They would all say "Hi Nan" in their friendly voices. I would then tell them the horrors of my addiction. How I could not go even one day without Certs®. I couldn't put the kids on the bus without Certs®; I couldn't even drive in the car without Certs®!!! I would beg for their help. They would all look at me. There would be no sympathy in their eyes.

On the way home from that meeting, with my butt still hurting where the guy kicked me, and my clothes all muddy from the puddle they threw me in out the front door, I would stop and buy a 24 pack of Certs®.

There is no hope for me.

14
Surveys and Telemarketing

We have just finished dinner. Three of the five children are quiet, which my husband and I consider a solid A on our child rearing report card. We sit down to discuss minimal house matters, such as the fact that we have not paid our mortgage in six months and the man came and knocked on the door today to throw us out of the house, so I hid myself and TJ in the bathtub for an hour or better. Just then the phone rings. We hate the phone ringing when we are trying to talk, because the chance to sit down and talk in our house comes with the same regularity as Haley's Comet. We are usually just passing by, grabbing coats, and screaming out where we are headed and when we will be back at home base. There are the rare occasions when we do get to have an adult conversation. I swear we have a pact not to use the words Barney, Blue, or Pokemon during these conversations.

Without a doubt, just when we get to the point where we can figure out how to stop hiding from the PSE&G meter reader, the phone rings. "Good evening, Ma'am," a pleasant enough voice on the other end of the phone says, "How are you this evening?" "I'm trying to figure out how to hide from the Public Service meter reader," I reply, "Got any ideas?" She politely chuckles. "We are conducting a survey . . ." I hear nothing else. I want to slam down the receiver in her stupid get-a-real-job ear, but I quickly remember the three-month stint I had done as a telephone solicitor. It was horrible; the worst three months of my life. If I am ever starving, and sleeping on a street corner wrapped in yesterday's newspaper to keep warm, and someone came up and offered me $100 an hour to solicit over the phone, I would pull my newspaper up over my head and go back to sleep. You could not pay me enough to do that kind of work again.

I feel very sorry for the people who have to do this kind of work and I tend to give them a few moments of my time. So I am going to have to hide from the meter reader again next month. At least I will feel as if I helped someone out, who would otherwise have had a phone slammed down on her or a shrill whistle blown in her ear. At the very least, she would have been called a name not befitting a dead animal, let alone a live person on the other end of the line.

The solicitor informs me that this survey will take no more than five minutes, at which time I set my oven timer and inform that if she goes over five minutes, I will hang up on her and she will have to hand in an incomplete. Of course, I know she will just dial back and promise me that she needs just a few more moments of my precious time. She informs me that her company desperately needs my opinion on constipation and its conse- quences. Now I know we need to get Mr. John Q. Public's opinion on what kind of underwear he prefers, which type of tobacco he would like to smoke and what kind of car he drives. However, it seems that every time a solicitor calls my house, it has some- thing to do with a bodily function, another planet or something that will cost the government tons of money to find out we did not need it in the first place, or that nobody cares about.

After discussing various very personal toilet habits with this woman (I felt we knew each other well enough to invite her over for Thanksgiving dinner), my timer has buzzed and I am about to hang up. She has said, "Just one more question" thirty seven times and I am really getting annoyed. I think she is about to finish this thing when she says, "Now I would like you to listen to some advertising campaigns for products to help with constipation. This will just take a few more minutes . . ." CLICK. I hang up. I guess she won't be joining us for Thanksgiving after all.

15
◯*Mom's Taxi*

I just got back from my third trip to the Mall today, and I am not finished. I still have to go back and pick everybody up. When I was younger and did not have any kids, I used to laugh at the signs on the back of the station wagons that said, "MOM'S TAXI". I really didn't understand what they meant. I am now living the nightmare.

My car has clocked more miles than the red eye to Florida. My husband calls it the Big Blue Bus, and I have a serious medical condition called gas ass. I feel like I never leave the car. Why am I paying a mortgage on my house? I live in the car anyway. At least my car is comfortable. We have a seven-passenger van and the driver's seat has the perfect imprint of my body, having been driving on it for the last six years.

Having five children, there is never any place in the house for the kids to have any peace and quiet. We won't even talk about MY lack of privacy. I have always told the kids I would be glad to drive them anywhere because if they have a friend over, I will not be able to stand the other four kids torturing the one who gets to have a friend over. For future reference, if you are planning on having kids, never tell them you will be glad to drive them anywhere. They will take you up on it and throw it in your face if you refuse to drive them somewhere just one time.

Of course, it is summer right now and gas ass flares up quite a bit during the summer months. I would get up in the morning; drive Erin to swim team practice. As soon as I get home, Shannon has to go to acting class. After I drop off Shannon at acting class, I pick Erin up from swimming practice. I then take Erin home and pick up Casey and Robby for swim lessons. After swim lessons, I take everybody home for a short period of time. Then there would be some complaining of boredom and how they never get to do anything. A friend would call. I would drive Robby to his friend's house and then his friend would have a sister Casey's age, so I drive back home and pick up Casey and take her to Robby's friend's house. About this time Shannon would be done acting class and I would pick her up and take her home. Shannon, being a teenager, would then absolutely have to go to the Mall, with five of her closest friends (this is the same child who two years ago could not buy a friend!).

So, off to the Mall we go. On the way back from the Mall, I pick up Robby and Casey at their friend's house and apologize to the mother for having to feed them as I forgot where they were. It is now time to pick up Shannon and her cronies from the Mall. After the seven stops to drop off all of her friends, I take Shannon home.

When I finally get home just to check my mail and restock the refrigerator, my husband asks if I would like to go out to dinner. Of course, fire is now shooting out of my gas ass as I run to the car for some peace and quiet with my husband, and perhaps a nice dinner. We run to McDonald's® and grab a bag of burgers for the children. They are thrilled.

As we make our way to our favorite restaurant, the car starts bucking and jumping. My husband slowly but cautiously asks, "Hon, did you remember to get gas today?"

Defeated once again, we walk home. I grab a burger out of the bag, drive my husband back up to pick up the car and come home. Now I am OUT OF GAS - for another day.

16
Getting Pulled Over

For most people, their daily routine goes off without a hitch. Well, I am not most people and on any given day, more than one hitch is usually thrown in. On this particular day, I am late taking my daughter to preschool. I get her and her little brother buckled into the car and off we go. As I said before, I am running late and driving down the road to my daughter's school. I am reviewing her manners with her, "Make sure to say please and thank-you", "don't pull any other little girl's hair", the usual, when I see the flashing lights in my rearview mirror. It is only then that I realize that siren I heard was for me.

Unless you are a repeat offender, or just plain don't care, the sight of those flashing lights is enough to make you, well, nervous, to say the least. I am now scared to death as I pull my van over to the side of the road. I am going over in my head what to say, be polite, stay calm, stop shaking. You would think I was carrying a vanload of cocaine. What's the worst that could happen? I'm pretty sure you don't have to do hard time for driving 35 miles an hour in a 25 mile per hour speed zone, but don't quote me on that. For all I know, I could get the cop that has a bug up his butt about short, fat, Irish women, and I'll end up selling myself for cigarettes in cell block eight.

Anyway, here comes Officer Ruin My Day. He asks to see my license. As I fumble for it in my wallet I realize my youngest son, Baby Houdini, has gotten out of his car seat and is standing up on the seat next to me, a fact that has not gone unnoticed by you-know-who, because Baby Houdini is yelling, "Hi cop. Are we going to jail?" "No son" he replies sounding exactly like Dudley Dooright, "but I need to talk to your mom now. You should be in your car seat." He then gives me that look that tells me he is definitely not on the side of short, fat, Irish women.

I show the officer my license, registration and insurance. Thank God I remembered to wipe the peanut butter off the insurance card when I found it near the toaster the other day. He asks if I know why he has pulled me over. I play stupid. He informs me that I was exceeding the speed limit by ten miles and was there a good reason for that? For a moment, I consider telling him that I was just beeped by the Vatican to let me know my audience with the Pope had just been granted and I had twenty minutes to get to the airport and hop the next plane to Rome. This would have been a plausible excuse except for the fact that I was going in the opposite direction of the airport.

I decide to come clean and tell him about my real crime. My daughter was late for preschool and she didn't want to lose her star. She was also very upset she might miss finger painting. I also assure him that my son was in a car seat when this little trip started out, and that someday he will see him on "Star Search" as an escape artist and he could say, "Hey, I remember that kid. I made his mom soil her upholstery with my siren one time."

He lets me go with a warning and tells me to be more careful next time. I thank him and ask him if he knows a good place to get the seats of my car cleaned.

17
⟲ The Argument

Everybody loves a good discussion. Most people even love a good argument. My children seem to thrive on it. They know they will eventually lose, because I would not have had five children if I were not absolutely sure not one of them would ever be able to pull the wool over my eyes. This statement, of course, coming from a woman who has yet to deal with adolescence, right? Or so they tell me.

Anyway, as I have said before, no two of our children are alike. So arguments always pose a great challenge, both to them and me. Our oldest child, Shannon, is our pre-adolescent, or as I prefer to think of her as, the child most likely to make me break all Ten Commandments in one day. I think she is up to making me break at least three on a good day, but she is determined. Our second child, another daughter, Erin, will turn on the water works and try to make us feel bad for her during an argument. She always throws little sayings in her argument like; "I never thought my own mother would talk to me that way" and I smirk because this one thinks she has me. Our third child, a boy, Robby, is still quite innocent and well behaved. The girls have yet to rub off on him but they are still holding out hope he will learn to be as argumentative as they can be. I hear tell it happens with boys more towards the times when they want to borrow the car, so I have Robby on my side for a few more years. Casey, our fourth child, a girl, and in kindergarten, is just learning to try and test our bounds, and has the art of whining down to a science. We are hoping to keep her on our side for a little while longer, before she breaks out and becomes an adolescent. Our youngest, TJ, well I think by the time he reaches the argumentative age I am just going to be too old and too tired to argue with him. I am really hoping he somehow gets a really good moral compass in his head, or else he is going to cost us a fortune in bail money.

Let's pick a topic for argument. Okay, I have just told all of the children they cannot watch television until they pick up all their toys or stuff. Shannon and Erin no longer have toys, they have "stuff". They are toys, but no one is allowed to know that. Anyway, that is the argument.

Of course the smart thing to do would be to pick up the toys or "stuff" and be done with it. Not this crowd. Robby will pick up his toys. Like I said, he has yet to break out of the "I want to please mommy and daddy mold." He however, sets boundaries for his cleaning. "I will pick up ten toys," he states, "and the girls have to do the rest, because they are not doing anything." I, being happy to have any toys at all picked up, agree to this plan. Hey, he was the first one to take a bite. He goes to watch television. TJ just cries because evidently there was a pattern to this mess, which Robby has just disturbed and his plan was to have every toy in the house, including the girl's "stuff", in this pile. He doesn't want to pick it up or have it disturbed, so the whole time I am trying to get this little mess cleaned up, he screams. His latest is to call everyone he is mad at an "idiot". He repeatedly screams "you idiot" in my ears as I carry him to the chair. I am still telling the girls to clean up their "stuff". Casey begins to whine, "This is too much stuff to pick up and I'm tired and I have a headache, and I am too little to pick up these things, etc." She just keeps whining as I tell her she cannot watch television until she does her share of the work. She calls me a slave driver and begins to start picking up one thing at a time, picking up a shoe with the same face Mankind has when he picks up Hulk Hogan. "I have asked you to pick a few things up, not upright the Leaning Tower of Pisa," I say to her. Again, she lists all the reasons, in a perfect pitch whine, why she should not be made to do such hard labor.

Erin of course, relies on the fact that no matter what they are doing, my two oldest girls cannot get along. She begins to tattle on Shannon, hoping I will say they cannot be in the same room together, and thereby she gets out of cleaning the room. Of course, being the intelligent woman that I am, I inform them that under no circumstances, including fire or flood, are they to speak to one another. They must clean in silence. Silence of course, means to pick at one another in a whisper until your mother hears you and comes at you with the kitchen broom. They do this until I hit them where it hurts most. I bellow, "No one is allowed to talk to their friends, either at the door, or on the telephone for one week." "Mom, please, we'll clean. Don't do that to us."

Now we come to Shannon. I guess I am just beginning to learn about adolescence, because this child is the very definition of "do the opposite of everything your parents say." She has slid into adolescence perfectly. Remember she was told to do one simple task, clean up her "stuff"! So far she has come up with thirty-seven reasons why she cannot possibly do this, along with a soliloquy on the perils of being the oldest of five children that would make Shakespeare seem illiterate. I then tell her how she could have had the entire house cleaned in the time and effort it took to tell me her tales of woe, and why can't she just do what she is told and not argue with me? Of course, guess what? Thirty-seven more reasons why she cannot do what she is told, and another monologue.

I think that pile of "stuff" sits there still.

18
⟲ It's Report Card Time

It is report card time again. This occurs four times during the school year and is the time when the parents find out exactly how their children are doing in school. Sometimes, the report card does not always jive with the children's version of their progress for the semester. For some reason, over the years, the children have yet to figure out that parents have to sign these report cards, so we will find out what is going on. My children could write their own Book Of Excuses for why the report card does not reflect what they have been telling me about their progress.

In our house we have a veritable melting pot of mentality. Shannon and Erin have the ability and do not use it; Robby is an anal retentive straight A student, Casey appears to be just as smart, but we all know kindergarten does not quite give an accurate assessment of one's future learning potential, and of course TJ - well let's just say I am already teaching him to say, "Would you like a hot dog to go with that Slurpee, sir?" We don't hold out much hope for the future of our generation.

Anyway, I usually start hinting about the report cards coming home for a week before they actually come home. Remember, I take my job as a parent seriously, and I would not miss an opportunity to tip the angst scale to its very limit. They start telling me how they have the worst teacher in the history of the public school system. Their teacher is a practicing witch. They are the only kid in the class whom the teacher picks on, etc. As I stated before, their Book Of Excuses could earn them quite a bit of money. I love it. I even pretend to sympathize and really make them believe I will buy every excuse they throw at me.

By the time the report cards come home, I have my children believing I am the only parent since Adam and Eve who will buy any story thrown at her. So of course, they willingly turn over the little piece of paper that will transform me into a screaming lunatic. They never learn, though, as is obvious from their report cards. Next report card they will fall for the same old routine.

I always start with the oldest and work my way down. I love each one of my children dearly and I treat them as individuals. Obviously with five children, you will see children with great ability and scholastic aptitude and children who can't put one foot in front of the other. Smart or challenged, I love every one of them.

Shannon is an average student, who does not always put her best foot forward. So when I see her report card, I am ecstatic with an A, overjoyed with a B, and satisfied with a C. I see no reason, however, to get a D in Spanish. Of course, I cannot speak Spanish, but it is a language. All you have to do is read the book and spit it out. There is very little brainpower used here. Of course, Shannon thinks her report card is great, since Spanish is not a major subject. "Didn't I do great, mom?" She sees that I am not happy and always loves to throw out, "So I am not as smart as Robby, you can't hold that against me." Mind you, I have, as yet, said nothing. They always hang themselves. I move on.

We come to Erin. Erin, I am told and it is obvious, is very bright, but would rather socialize than do her work. Hence, her grades fall due to missed homework and lack of study time, etc. She hands me her report card, and goes to comb her hair. She has failed Math. Okay, I hate Math too, but I never failed it. I wasn't allowed to fail anything. Of course, she tries to tell me about her teacher, Beelzebub, and how she hates her and picks on her, yada, yada, yada. I listen and then tell her she is grounded until the next marking period, and we will try to get an exorcism performed on her teacher.

Robby is sad because he got all As and one B. He tells me he is going to work harder and bring that B up to an A. I think this is God trying to tell me that I am not the very essence of a bad mother. Casey of course, in kindergarten, is just interested in what the report card says. She cannot read it and therefore is assuming that her teacher has filled her report card with the wonders of my Mensa candidate. Why can't kindergarten report cards have the regular letter grades? They did when I was in kindergarten and all we did was finger-paint. Now, they do letters and numbers, addition, subtraction. Why does a kindergarten report cards always have to have M for mastered, P for progressing and N for not yet introduced? If it is not yet introduced, leave it off the report card. I have enough report cards to look at. If they have mastered it, give them an A, if they are progressing, a C, etc. I really believe the school system is really trying to keep us confused, so we will just keep voting for larger budget.

Report card time, at least for this semester, is over. Punishments have been handed out as necessary. A few Slurpees have been bought as bribes. I mark my calendar for the next report card distribution. I can't wait to hear the excuses next time!

19
School is Out for Summer

The weather gets warmer. The grass is starting to look like the wilds of Africa. Final exams are approaching. Looks like the kids are going to be out of school soon. Oh Joy! Oh Bliss! Oh S! #@! You can just see all of the teachers grinning. They have that little bounce in their step and that look in their eyes that says, "See you later, suckers!!! I am getting rid of you and I am going to spend my summer with a three-month hangover! Good luck in juvenile hall!" With that thought in mind, they send the little darlings home for the summer.

I, for one, think that teachers should have partial legal custody of the children they teach. They would have to take them on Wednesdays and every other weekend through the summer. After all, nine months isn't nearly enough time to get to know these kids. Hell, as their parents we have known them for years and we still can't figure them out. But alas, they send the children back to us, leave the school and make a B line for the liquor store or the shore, or as far away as they can go for the next three months, to rest up for the next school year.

Anyway, school has been out for all of three minutes and my children are bored to tears. Of course I suggest some great out of school activities. "You could start out the summer right by cleaning your room, or at least making a path to your bed so you can find it at night." They roll their eyes. "Well" I continue,

"You could clean up the yard so people would stop coming up and asking if this is the city dump!" Their eyes roll further back into their heads. Undaunted, I then suggest the unthinkable, "We could always go to the library and refresh your memory of the English language." Their eyes fall out of their sockets.

After we spend the next few days replacing their eyeballs, we decide to join the local swim club. Everybody thinks this is a great idea, except of course, for me. I realize for them this means socializing with friends instead of forging that path to their beds, or increasing their brainpower at the library. Shannon will want to stay home and talk on the phone. Erin will spend the entire summer perfecting just the right way to walk past the boy she likes and Robby and TJ will master just the right cannonball splash to make all the other parents at the swim club hate me. For me, it means getting nothing accomplished, as well as triple the laundry because now I will have to wash towels and bathing suits every day. I will also have to grow a few extra sets of eyes if I want to keep track of only the children that belong to me. The husbands get to escape this phenomenon as they have real jobs. My husband wishes he had all day to sit around the swim club. I wish I had a 40-hour a week job, instead of the 168 hours I put in each week, but that's another story.

I get the added bonus of spending the better part of my summer at the baby pool. This of course, is the smaller pool at the swim club, where the babies have to stay until they are out of diapers. It is just like the Rugrats, only with water all around. Since TJ has decided that he is going to college in diapers, this is the place

I am relegated to year after year. The mothers in this area make small talk about baby things, breastfeeding, (a regular attraction at the baby pool), and the fact that we cannot wait to graduate to the big pool.

We all sit around the baby pool, waiting for one of the babies to poop in the pool. Of course, this happens once in a while and there is always a 25% chance it is my child. When this happens, the pool guy comes in and makes all the kids get out of the pool. This does not make for a happy little group of Rugrats. They can't go in the water because, in order to kill the poop germs, the pool guy has to dump enough chlorine in the pool to burn holes in their tender skin. So now we all have to wait for the chlorine to "burn off" the water, which takes about an hour, or in Rugrats terms, three lifetimes. All the angry mothers and sniveling brats sit and stare at me 25% of the time.

I have suggested that we just replace the water in the baby pool with cat litter. Then, when one of the babies has an accident, we just use a big scoop and continue to play. They suggested I move to a small island, shave my head, and join a cult selling flowers in the airport. I can't wait for school to start again!!

20
House Cleaning

I hate everybody out there who has a kitchen floor you could eat off of because it is so clean. You can eat off of my kitchen floor because there is enough food there for you. There are also plenty of bacteria so I wouldn't recommend it. I am willing to say here and now, without any embarrassment; well maybe a little embarrassment, that I am a lousy housekeeper. I am lots of fun at parties, as long as they are at someone else's house. I am a great mom, or at least I think so. All the kids in the neighborhood call me the "cool" mom. This means that I don't care if they eat in the living room and I am always available to drive them to the mall.

But back to the matter at hand. Housecleaning is a stupid, stupid thing to do. I hate it, every part of it. Oh, don't get me wrong. I love it when the house is clean; I just hate to be the one to do it. And, I am totally sick of hearing other women say things like, "Oh today I have to do my windows, inside and out." Why bother cleaning the outside of the windows? Is this not why God made rain? I have also heard more ridiculous things said by obsessive compulsive cleaners like, "Oh, I have to put away the winter clothes and take out the summer clothes." In my house, all clothes are kept in all drawers throughout the seasons. The drawers don't shut anyway so it doesn't matter how much stuff you pile into them.

Here's one of my favorites, "I spent all morning doing my baseboards," like I should applaud or something. What the hell is a baseboard? Do I have them in my home? Then there's, "I emptied all the kitchen cabinets this morning, got rid of all the old spices, and relined the shelves." Correct me if I am wrong but do these women have nothing better to do? Are they doing this during Oprah? Perish the thought. If Maury has two headed transsexuals on, I am not, I repeat NOT, going to reline the shelves. Who gives a rat's you-know-what about the bottom of the shelves? My glasses and dishes don't complain. I have never had a spice and dish rebellion from my kitchen cabinets. If they don't mind, neither do I. The glasses are clean when you put them in the cabinets and then you wash them before you put them away. As far as I am concerned they are sterilized, no need to line the shelves with anything. As far as getting rid of old spices, no way. You never know when you are going to be cooking something and need a dash of tamarind or chopped cloves, and won't that lady be sorry she tossed them? Not me. Every spice you can think of is shoved into that cabinet somewhere. Never let it be said that I am not prepared.

Some people like to "clean out the closets". What the hell for? You are just going to end up with a lot of junk on the floor. At least if it is in the closet, nobody can see it. The motto I live by is this - If you can't see junk, it doesn't exist.

There are people who have cleaning schedules. Vacuuming on Mondays, Wednesdays and Fridays. Windows on Tuesdays and Thursdays. Wash the floors every other day, laundry daily, etc. I have a schedule as well. Vacuum when somebody calls to say they are coming over. I usually use a Shop Vac® because all the crap on my floor doesn't fit through those little nozzles and beater bars of regular vacuum cleaners. Why don't they make vacuum cleaners with openings the size of say, heating ducts? Now there's a vacuum that could handle my house! Anyway, back to my schedule. Windows when you can't see outside. Wash the floors when your feet stick to them. Laundry when everybody is out of underwear. See, my way is much less an anal way to keep the house clean. My husband comes in from work, steps over the toys, kicks the jackets out of the way and makes his way across the sticky kitchen floor to give me a kiss.

I don't even want to begin to discuss the knick-knack crowd. I hate to walk into someone's house and see shadow boxes. These, of course, are those annoying little boxes with a dozen or so cubby holes the size of Oreo® cookies, and you put cute little "miniature" things in them like thimbles or mugs with names on them. This is another major waste of time that could be spent watching trash television. If I had a shadow box, it would look like I picked it up at Boris Karloff's garage sale. It would have say, a shattered mug, a bent thimble, a doll head, a Hot Wheel® car without wheels, some cat hair, a small container of fennel seed (so it didn't fit in the spice cabinet), and other interesting trinkets that I tripped over or stepped on and needed a place to put them. Even if I tried to make a shadow box of, say, "spoons from around the world", there would be one morning when the dishwasher didn't get loaded and all the spoons would have to replace the dirty cereal spoons and I would, hence, have to find more replacement things for my shadow box. This is way too much work!

Okay, all you stencil people out there, you really have a lot of catching up to do. I bet you haven't seen a good lesbian fight on Springer for at least a year. You really need a break. Stencil people spend their time stenciling things like vines, fruit or geometric shapes to border the tops of their walls, just for a different look. Well, guess what? I have stencils too. Just the other day I went into the girls' room to find their names written on the walls, in various colors, with various tools. Casey even stenciled her bureau and, of course, one small stencil on the ceiling. She climbed on the top bunk for this art project. They all say "CASEY". I tried to tell her that in her life of graffiti, she would probably be better off not using her own name to give herself away but she seems to like this particular "stencil".

TJ prefers to take whatever writing or scraping tool he has in his hand and make designs of his own. We have some wallpaper scratched out in the hallway. There is a big pencil swirl in the living room and the white oven in the kitchen now has hot orange highlighter designs upon it. Now wouldn't this house make a great abstract art exhibit? I am trying, as you read this, to talk my husband into pulling the oven out of the wall so I can take it to the museum the next time an Andy Warhol exhibit is showing.

Casey and TJ will always draw on themselves when they run out of wall and bureau space. By the time I get all the marks off their bodies they look as if they have survived a cougar attack because the black, blue, green, or whatever color markers leave little red lines on their skin. When I was younger my mother used to tell me and my sisters that we would get lead poisoning if we drew all over ourselves. It stopped us immediately. My kids see this as an opportunity to get out of going to school and begin yet another design that I will have to scrub off in the bathtub that evening.

Let's get to the most hated of clean freaks, the outside clean people. These are the people who landscape their yards and vacuum their garages. These are people in serious need of a life. The day I vacuum a garage is the day Martha Stewart comes a-knocking, and we all know what I am going to do to her! I finally had to hire a lawn service. One day we lost one of the kids in the grass it was so high. We were getting ready to apply for a tax break and call our yard swampland (protected environ-mental property), when one of our garage-vacuuming neighbors, or maybe it was the whole neighborhood, complained to the township about our yard. We got a letter stating that if we did not cut our grass and clean up our yard, they were going to do it for us and add the bill to our taxes.

I was outraged. I wrote the township a letter explaining that I had five children, my husband and I were both working full time, and did these people really expect I would not have a yard full of toys? Somehow I had to keep these children quiet while Montel grilled the teenagers who beat their parents and robbed them for drug money. The township replied stating that a seat

72

from a van, the front end of a Lincoln Continental, an empty industrial wire spool and various broken pieces of lawn furniture did not constitute "toys" and we had to clean it up. So we cleaned up the yard and hired a lawn service. Mind you, my husband does know how to cut the grass. He just doesn't have the time, what with work and his Hot Wheel® hobby! DON'T EVEN GET ME STARTED!!!!

Anyway, to all those neighbors out there who ever complained to the township about our yard, I have just one thing to say. I bet I am more fun at a party, so let's have one at your house. You know the one with the vacuumed garage and the bonsai trees out front.

21
ℰ Barbies™

If you are female, or if you have a daughter, granddaughter, niece or sister, you have undoubtedly dabbled in Barbie™ playtime at some point in your life. Okay, Barbie™ has a certain purpose in society. That is to keep little girls from screaming and whining about anything and everything. However, if you look at Barbie™ over the years, how she has changed many times over; big boobs, little boobs, small waist, a little girth, bendable legs, and movable anything, one thing remains constant. If a Barbie™ comes into our house, she will be naked in less than one hour. The market for Barbie™ clothes MUST be the biggest Fools' Gold market there ever was. We have a couple of hundred Barbies™ in our house and not one of them has clothes on.

My girls are 5, 10, and 13 as I write this. Even at those diverse ages, Barbie™ never has any clothes on. Of course the oldest daughter tries. She likes to look at the fashions and even purchase one or two that catch her eye. She will dress Barbie™ up and attempt to put her hat and shoes on. Barbie™ has a really high arch problem with her feet and shoes never seem to stay on. If you have no intention of using Crazy Glue® to keep her shoes on, do yourself a favor and don't even try to put shoes on Barbie™. Let her high arches go "au naturelle".

Anyway, Shannon dresses Barbie™ up. She may even join in a little play with Erin, who of course, always has to be Ken, since

74

Shannon says so. Ken doesn't always seem to be as naked as Barbie™ even though he has only one swimsuit. He seems to be allowed to keep his clothes on. They will play for a while. Ken and Barbie™ eventually get married. They live happily ever after and Barbie™ playtime is done for these two. They put the dolls down. This is where the problem is. If you really want to keep a well-dressed Barbie™, you have to carry her around constantly. As soon as you let your guard down and put her down some-where, Casey is waiting, with her pudgy little hands just itching to undo those buttons. You know, the little buttons from Munchkin Land. The person who made those tiny little buttons, and the hook and eye closures for Barbie™ clothes is now bounc-ing off her rubber walls in a well-guarded sanitarium. Can you imagine spending all day making buttons you can't even see, let alone fitting them through a hole you can't see either?

Ah hah! But Casey can see them and she does not like them. Those little buttons and hook and eye closures keep Barbie™ from being naked. If Barbie™ is not naked, how can Casey draw all over her in magic marker? She must be naked so that phase II of Casey's plan can be carried out.

Phase II consists of giving each Barbie™ in our house her own little characteristic that sets her apart from every other Barbie™ of that type. For example, Malibu Barbie™ quickly transforms into Malibu Magic Marker Barbie™ with Casey's quick hands and a few colored magic markers she has stolen from her sisters. Tropical Hair Barbie™ easily becomes Tropical Tangle Hair Barbie™, as she ends up with real styling gel in her hair, which

75

turns to cement if not washed out. Casey will make sure nobody finds this Barbie™ until her hair becomes plastered to her naked body.

Ballerina Barbie™ dances only a few steps before she becomes Barbie™ One Foot, as her feet are jointed and easier to remove than the one-piece-leg Barbies™. Her career as a ballerina is quickly sidelined by Casey's desire to chew off one foot. I really do feed these children, I swear! Princess Rapunzel Barbie™ in our house has had the distinction of becoming Barbie™ No Hair. Why she needed her hair cut so short that you could see the round, plastic bald spot in the middle of her head I do not know but this Barbie™ needs a doll clinic, quick!

Any jointed Barbie™ will need artificial limb replacements by the time Casey is done with her. Any Barbie™ who came into the house with a full head of hair will either lose it or it can be found sticking out of the bathtub drain, since all the Barbies™ in our house need to take a bath with Casey EVERY night.

I suppose this pastime is okay since it makes Barbie™ a little more life-like. I mean let's face it. If women had the comparable measurements of a Barbie™ doll, we would not be able to balance ourselves on our spindly legs while our ample tops dragged our faces to the ground. Oh men would look, alright, but all they would see is our butts with little "B"s painted all over them, because we wouldn't be able to upright ourselves - how attractive!!!

22
The Cereal Aisle

I love to go to the grocery store. I arm myself with my double coupons; get a babysitter and head to the store. I guess at this point in my life I should consider it my "night out". Anyway, one of my favorite aisles is the cereal aisle. It should be. Three of the five kids will only eat cereal for dinner three nights a week, so I usually have to buy between five and eight boxes a week. It is a great challenge to me to find the best deal for my money, something edible, yet cheap. I am on a mission.

I will not spend $4.00 for a box of cereal. The people who own cereal companies should not be allowed to sleep at night for charging $4.00 for a box of sugar hunks. The natural cereals are more expensive, but the truth is, if I were going to eat one of them, I would just go out and munch on a tree for free. They taste the same. My kids would throw this stuff in the trash as soon as look at it. The very names of some of those cereals make me stay away. There is one called Sprouts Seven. Seven what, heads? Exactly what is this cereal sprouting? I am certainly not going to open the box and look to find out. The only things that I have ever seen sprouted in my life were gray hair on my head and weeds on the lawn.

Of course there are the cereals that might as well just say on the box, "Buy me. I will keep your children up and running for days!" Chocolate cereal with chocolate marshmallows. The nutritional content of this cereal is about the same as if you ate the box, zero. It is a box of sugar, flavored with chocolate. It turns the milk to chocolate milk and eats holes in the kid's teeth. They will beg for this cereal every time you shop. Go figure!

If you have kids, forget any cereal that starts with "bran" or "gran" as in "granola". The kids think these cereals taste just like wallpaper and they would not be far from the truth. Oh the cereal companies try and spice these cereals up by adding nuts and fruits, the names of which I don't know. Where are they grown? What the hell is a boysenberry? If you could get your kids to eat this, good for you. If not, don't buy it. It will just grow weevils in your cabinet and you will have a whole new problem.

Corn flakes, everybody's favorite. In my house, no one will eat them unless a cup of sugar is poured onto them before the milk, thereby negating the nutritional value of this cereal. However, without the sugar, corn flakes taste like wood chips. Then there is the cereal that is supposed to have the nutty taste. They should rename this cereal "Fish Tank Gravel". One bite of this stuff and you are flying over to your dentist to have your broken tooth fixed. Who in the name of all that is good and Holy, ever thought of putting fish tank gravel in a box and selling it as cereal? It is a sick world.

Oatmeal is in the cereal aisle. I love oatmeal. I don't think you want to know what my kids call it. On occasion, I have been able to get them to try some oatmeal, after I load it up with brown sugar and syrup.

At the end of the cereal aisle is the new growing fad, cereal bars. These are supposed to be a quick breakfast, if you are on the go. What they are is mashed up cereal with some fruit jammed in the middle. When you are in a hurry, just slam one of these down and you are on your way, nourished for the day. That is if you don't barf it up on your way for eating so fast. You could choose a granola bar, but there is that "gran" prefix again and you know what that means. Someone could have put some of that fish tank gravel in it, so if you eat it, make sure you are in the vicinity of your dentist's office.

23
ℰ Going To The Mall

I hate the mall. Okay, I loved the mall when I was a teenager and for a while my mother used it as a forwarding address for anyone who tried to contact me at home. However, once the tables turned and I am the one paying the bills, driving the carpools, and taking three to six screaming adolescents to run through a mall, for one second I cannot remember the reason I loved it. It is a horrendous place.

I walk into a mall and I can immediately feel the gravitational pull from every store on my wallet. The kids run in every direction as if there was a giant fireball about to run up behind us. They absolutely MUST have one thing from every store and kiosk in the mall before we go home, thereby adding to the expense of a day at the mall, one U Haul rental truck to get all the "stuff" home that they will not be able to find the next morning.

The most important trip of the day is to the clothing store. This is the place where everybody-has-'em pants are sold as well as anybody who is anybody shirts, gotta-have-'em shoes and must have accessories. They will spend their allowance, as well as the allowance of Bill Gate's children in this store. For about a week's salary you will be able to walk out of this store with a purse and a shirt that would fit a small Chihuahua. These are definite necessities for all teenagers.

Your next stop will be the store that has all the smelly stuff in it, such as body sprays that have names like Freesia, but smell like they should have names like Last Week's Diaper Pail. They really don't smell that bad. It is just that teenage girls have mistaken these light sprays for bath soap and spray them head to toe at least three to four times a day. Maybe these are "cootie" sprays, but when we were younger we had to pretend to spray them on ourselves. Now they have actually invented one and I guarantee this stuff will keep all boys, with and without "cooties", away within a ten-mile radius.

There is the absolutely necessary earring and bracelet store. I have one daughter who does not even have her ears pieced, but she needs to go into this store and pick out something "fuzzy", like a fuzzy pen, fuzzy diary or fuzzy key chain. How have we survived without these must-have items? I hear the local schools have decided to give out "fuzzy" demerits if you have too many fuzzy things hanging from your locker or backpack.

One important stop along your journey will be the music store. Let them go in by themselves and save you the headache. Even if you did like to listen to loud music when you were younger, this is not the place for you. What they listen to is called "music", but believe me, it is the farthest thing from music. In this store you will find CDs from groups whose names translate into things like We Worship Satan on a Regular Basis or something like that. If you can't understand a damn thing these groups are saying, the kids probably can't either, but everyone else is buying these CDs, so your kids will have to have them too.

I could stop at the food court except for the fact that the only thing an adolescent eats is lettuce and at the salad place you will pay more for a bowl of lettuce then you would for a small, compact car. You could get a cup of coffee, if you could decide on which kind to get. It used to be that you bought a cup of coffee and sat down and drank it. Now, one needs to decide if you would like a latte, café cooler, cappuccino, and on. Even if you could decide what kind you wanted, you then have to decide which flavor you want it in, of which there are 24 of each kind. What ever happened to the good old days when a cup of coffee was a cup of coffee, and it costs less than a three-piece suit?

Of course there is always the store that looks like Jim Morrison created it, and probably is still alive and lives in the back of it. This is the store with the beaded curtains, lava lamps and posters of Farrah Fawcett, only with raunchier and more naked women on the posters. They sell incense in these stores, which immediately makes me sneeze and the kids look at me as if I have just ruined the karma of the entire experience this store has just created for them. I go wait outside where the other "dork" parents are sitting, while the kids browse through boob key chains and things with other sexual innuendo. They come out with their faces all red, insisting they don't like that store and they won't go in there again. Yeah, right.

We then always have to make a pit stop at the pet store. I hate this because all five of my children and whatever other children we have taken on this journey, are begging me to buy a puppy. Now, I like puppies as much as the next guy, but if I am going to pay $800.00 to clean up poop, I will sign myself into a sanitarium right now, if you know what I mean. I assure the kids one of these days we will see a stray and take him in and he will be our pet for life. They moan and groan. We move on.

I have to confess, I do enjoy going to the Mall to see Santa. I am one of those obnoxious mothers who dresses her kids up to the nines to get a three second picture on Santa's lap. The kids still get the biggest kick out of it. However, this little mall trip takes a total of twenty minutes, including line-waiting time. You see, I am a seasoned Santa line-waiting mom. I always make sure we go on an off day at an off time, which translates into a weeknight when Santa is about to go back to his workshop. He may be tired, but he looks good on film. We get in line, get on his lap, get a picture, read our lists, jump off his lap, grab our candy cane and head right back out the door. I tell the kids if we don't do it that way, Santa will think we are going to shop and buy things that his elves could make so much better and it would upset him. They run for the door.

24
⚬ Organized Sports

Well, here's a category I am just starting to learn about, as the children get older. I have to say I would rather see my children join organized crime than organized sports. The people who "organize" the sports should really get a life, not mine, but someone's.

It's time for Little League baseball sign ups. My son is now seven and can play Little League. I am totally against this as I never had a brother and would be real pressed to tell you what a baseball looks like, but my son is convinced this is the only thing he ever wants to do as long as he lives, so we allow him to sign up for Little League. This was one of the biggest mistakes we have made as parents so far.

At sign ups there are men in baseball type attire, looking like they are sizing my son up for a multimillion-dollar contract with the Phillies. I start to say, "He is seven!" My husband tells me to be quiet and looks at them as if to say, "What do you think? 40 million over ten years, you can have him!" I am appalled. We then proceed to pay them the rest of the money we have in our bank account so that my son can now wear pants that I can tell will not last through the first practice, and have a tee-shirt with his name on it, and of course, a number. A number on a tee shirt is to a seven-year-old boy what a large-breasted woman is to Hugh Hefner, you just gotta have one.

These men proceed to tell us that over the next few months we will be required to bring our son to every practice and game. He will need cleats, a pair of shoes with spikes in them. I shudder thinking of the holes I will be able to count in his little brother's head from these shoes. We need to buy baseball socks. I had to laugh. My husband shoots me that "Please don't let them know we have no idea what is going on here" look. Regular socks are not good enough for Little League. You have to purchase baseball socks from a sporting goods store, to the tune of four times what you would normally pay for socks for the entire family.

The man behind the table looks at my son and says to him, "So you wanna play baseball, do ya?" I am thinking if he starts yelling at my kid, I am going to buy myself a pair of cleats and make road maps in his forehead. "Can you hit?" he asks. My son looks down at his feet. "Can he hit?" I say, "His brothers and sisters have the bruises to prove it!" My husband puts his head in his hands. The coach continues, "Can you run?" "Can he run?" I am getting excited, "He spilled an entire gallon of milk on the floor the other morning and before I finished screaming, I think he was in the next town!" My husband escorts me out to the car and tells me he will no longer provide for the children and me if I show my face in that room again.

What did I do wrong? I was only trying to help my son. I think my husband stayed behind to negotiate a contract. Well, little did I know this was only the beginning. We get to the first practice. My son is already disappointed because he did not get to wear his number shirt to practice, it is for games only. I offered to paint a number on a shirt for him so that he could wear it to practice. He cried. I can't win.

It is time for the first game. He has his number shirt on. He begged me to stay home. Somehow, my very presence embarrasses him or maybe it is the fact that I have baseball paraphernalia saying, "GO ROBBY" all over it on every free space on my body. I go anyway. I want to see my son play ball.

The boys line up to hit. I, for one, could not hit the broad side of a barn with one of those big blow up balls you win on the boardwalk, but these kids can hit the baseball. My son hits the ball—far. I am amazed. Who would have thought it? The biggest sport his father and I have ever participated in was to see which one of us could stay on the couch the longest without having to get up to go to the bathroom. We figured we would not have athletes in the family. Of course, his grandfather has taken all the credit for the fact that my son is a good baseball player.

It is a good thing my son is good at this. The kids who are not-so-good baseball players get lectures the likes of which I have not heard since my Catholic high school days when we all made fun of the sex education book. These coaches are enthusiastic, or more to the point, insane. They are screaming and yelling at seven-year-old boys. "You couldn't hit a baseball if it stopped short in front of your nose!" the coach screams at one whimpering seven year old. "Turtles run faster than you do," he screams at another. I am thinking, "Where are these kid's parents? They must be out buying their cleats to walk all over these coaches!!"

I am told this is pretty much normal behavior for Little League coaches. They get very intense during the season and want the boys to learn the importance of teamwork, endurance and how hard work pays off. I'm figuring these guys could take care of our military crises. Just send them over to wherever we are warring and tell them to start a Little League team. End of war, period.

25
◯ The Perennial Diet

I have been dieting for better than one third of my life. I can honestly say I have lost a lot of weight. Of course, I always find it again. It does not like to be away from my body for very long. It is as if we have bonded and there is no way it is ever going to leave the nest for good. Not that I haven't tried to send it packing.

I wish I had invented the diet industry. I could be eating fat out of wagons being served by my maids by my private pool, which of course, would only hold me. But, who cares because my mansion would have a twenty-foot high solid black fence so no one could see my Weeble family and me.

The truth is I've tried them all, and for the most part, they work. They just don't work forever. If someone could make up a diet where you really could eat anything you wanted and still lose all the weight you wanted – now there would be somebody smoking big cigars! But the truth is, in order to lose weight, you have to stop eating as much, or at least in the way that you are now, or at least the way I am now.

I tried the liquid diet. This diet really did work, except that I began to go through "chew" withdrawal. I really needed something to chew. If I chewed on the children, I would go to jail. I almost went and bought some dog toys. They seem to last a long time. But then I figured they probably had some chemicals in them, and I don't need any more chemicals then I already have in my body. I had to take vitamins every day and once a week I had to go to the doctor's office to get a vitamin shot. It worked great for a while. I lost almost thirty pounds. I started to get suspicious that this diet would not work forever when I started nibbling on the magazines in the doctor's office and the people started looking at me funny. I stopped that diet and guess what? I found that weight again, and a few extra pounds that were traveling with it.

I went to Weight Watchers™. I loved Weight Watchers™. At the meetings the instructor was very "up" and very positive and always had a "fat" story that really made me believe she was in the same boat as me. Well, she was not in the same boat I was. She had already lost her weight. I was still carrying mine around. She told us that it was not easy, a fact I think most of us already knew. We were here, weren't we? We weighed in. Again, I did really well for the first couple of weeks. After a few weeks, I would go in and take off my rings so that I would show at least some weight loss. The instructor never really yelled. She would say things like, "Are you doing the things the book says?" Of course I would answer, "Yes." Of course, she knew I was lying. When it got too uncomfortable to go to Weight Watchers™, i.e. I had no more jewelry to shred, I stopped going. I found that weight again as well.

I tried a Christian weight loss group. I really liked the group. There was a group of about ten women and we would support each other, both in our faith and in our weight loss journey. The facilitator had the meetings at her house. She had a scale in the kitchen and we would just go in and weigh ourselves. We never told anybody how much we weighed or how much we lost or gained. We had to keep a diary and read Bible passages daily. We would discuss the Bible passages. The Bible study was great. Let me just say, my marriage got stronger, I was nicer to my children and my relationship with my sisters was great. I really did not lose a lot of weight. Maybe God has another plan for me. I mean, if He really meant for me to be skinny, He would have made me skinny. So I have stopped making the diet industry richer and have decided to do God's work. I am raising a great family. I will eat whatever I want and if it be His will I will be buried someday in a piano case.

26
Birthday Parties

I just picked my daughter up from a birthday party. It was a carnival. I don't mean a little carnival. I mean a carnival. There were face painters, sand artists, at least seven different games and tickets for prizes that ranged from rings to complete art sets. Pizza was delivered by the truckful. There were barrels of soda, popcorn, pretzels, etc. There were rented tables set up and at least 50 five year olds running around having a grand old time. I'm figuring for what mommy and daddy paid for this little "get together" they could have gone to Cancun and sent their daughter a birthday postcard.

I think this is a sign of the times. We live in an area of New Jersey that is up and coming. My family lives in the house I grew up in. My husband and I are both from this town. When we got married, we moved about ten miles away from here. After my mom passed away, we moved into the house where I grew up and that is where we live today. When I was a kid, this section of our town was considered "nice", however with all the larger homes sprouting up in our town, we are becoming the middle section of town. The median income in our town has gone way up and we just kept having kids. I guess we should have invested our extra $30.00 a year over the last couple of years, but we usually just went out to dinner or something like that.

Anyway, our neighborhoods have soared past us in the income brackets and hence, our children get invited to carnivals instead of birthday parties. This is both embarrassing and ridiculous. My son has been to birthday parties where there were team members autographing things, hockey parties at the rink where the Flyers practice, etc. My girls have been to dress up parties, where I had to actually go buy them new dresses to attend, nail parties where manicurists show and up and give each girl a set of artificial nails, and parties with DJs. I cannot keep up the pace.

I have tried to come up with an inexpensive way to throw a cute party for any one of the kids. They were not interested in having their friends watch daddy repair a dented fender for two hours. They were also not interested in having me dress up as Cher and sing a medley of Cher tunes. I refuse to go to Chucky Cheese® (I believe that huge mouse is giving subliminal messages to children to have their parents shell out some more money to purchase plastic spiders for outrageous prices). My children would not be caught dead at a McDonald's® party and under no circumstances am I inviting 40 to 50 well-to-do kids to my small, unpretentious home. My children would rather be subject to another cleaning session of their rooms.

Why can't a bunch of kids just get together and throw cake at each other and play musical chairs? When did birthday parties get so out of hand? Maybe what my children need to do is play a rousing game of "Pin The Life on Mommy!"

27
Buying A New Car

My husband and I took the kids out with us to buy a new dryer. Our old one had just given up the ghost, or maybe it was just too full from eating all of our old socks. Anyway, we are driving down the highway with the five kids and our new dryer in the back of our van. We pass one of the many car dealerships along the highway and my husband gets one of his bright ideas, "Let's just go in and take a look." Now I am no expert, but take my advice. If your spouse ever says these words to you, immediately have him or her pull the car over and you take over and drive yourselves right home. Otherwise you will live my nightmare and if you have been reading this book intently, you are probably by now, kissing the ground your kids throw their clothes on that you do not have my life.

Be that as it may we pull into the car lot. My sons are looking at this place as if were a big Hot Wheel® garage and these are all just bigger cars to play with. My oldest daughter is looking bored as usual, and pouring over the latest issue of a teen magazine. Of course, number two announces she has to go number one. Before we can release the latch on the van, a well-dressed salesman is in our faces, literally. I think all car salesman are wired with beepers that go off as soon as you pull onto the lot, so they can get to you and talk you into buying a car you cannot afford. You are signing on the dotted line before you know what hit you.

My husband gets out of the car and the man extends his hand and introduces himself, "Hello, my name is Ray and you are . . . " "Bob" my husband answers. Now to the best of my knowledge this is the first time either one of us has ever laid eyes on Ray, and yet he is talking as if he were the best man in our wedding. "What a beautiful family you have" Ray begins. "Thank you" I say, "Do you have a bathroom?" He motions towards the show-room and I trot off with number two to go number one, leaving Bob and his new best friend, Ray, to chat, along with the other four children and a lot full of brand new cars. By the time I get back approximately two minutes later, the car lot now looks akin to the monkey house at the zoo. The four children I left in Bob and Ray's care are now jumping or hanging off of different new cars that we cannot afford. I think Bob and Ray are planning on joining a bowling league together.

Ray walks over to me, "Nan, pleased to meet you, my name is Ray." I am thinking to myself, "Not when my crew gets done with you, your name will be mud." I smile. I realize I am not in the best of moods. Watching your children scratch and dent $100,000 worth of cars will do that to a person. I'm tired, I'm hungry and I don't want to see my kids destroy a second showroom in one day. Remember the dryer? I think we got such a good deal on it just so we would leave. "Bob here tells me you might be interested in a new van" Ray starts. I want to say, "Did Bob also tell you he left his brain back at the dryer store?" but I am polite. I resign myself to the fact that we are going to be looking at new cars. "Well you are in luck . . ." Ray's voice trails off as he begins to regale me on what a great time it is to buy a new car, with all the rebates and added extras. I pretend to be mildly interested. Bob pretends to be mildly intelligent.

Three hours later I have had it. I have been to the bathroom twelve times with various children, looked at over twenty cars, filled out a credit application that I am certain will be turned down, and I am starting to hate Ray. I'm glad he wasn't in our wedding. He starts to put the hard sell on us, throwing in another option. If we stay here long enough, I think we may be able to get a condo in Florida out of this guy. Bob is starting to harden, deciding that we are not going to buy a new car right now, but he would still like to go bowling with Ray, if he is free. Ray then states that we should take the van home for the weekend to see if we like it. We are sick of hearing Ray beg and plead so we say okay, we will take the van home for the weekend. Ray is ecstatic. He thinks he has us now. Can his commission really be worth all of this? I go to get my bags from our van, when I realize we have a dryer in the back of our van that needs to go home with us. I walk back over and timidly say, "Uh, Bob, what about the dryer?" Bob and Ray are exchanging phone numbers now and Bob is explaining to Ray that we were just coming from buying a new dryer. I continue, "We can't leave the dryer here. We will get Ray's car all wet, I won't be able to dry the laundry" I look at Ray, "unless of course that is another option you can throw in." I am getting sarcastic again. I hate when I do that.

Ray comes up with the bright idea of getting two guys to come

95

out and move the dryer from our van to our "weekend tryout" van. NOW - I know we are not going to buy this van. Bob knows we are not going to buy this van. The credit companies know they are not going to lend us the money to buy this van, but Ray is relentless. He goes to get somebody to move the driver.

"Bob, do you like this van?" I ask my husband. "It's all right," he says. "Well it had better be more than all right, because if you let Ray and his henchmen move my new dryer from our van to this van, it is going to be your new address!!!" Bob quickly shuffles the monkeys back into our old van, the one with the dryer in it, and we drive away, without saying goodbye to Ray. I guess he'll have to go bowling with the next sucker who pulls onto the lot.

28
∽ Going To Atlantic City

I have to say I love to gamble. I love to gamble so much that if I had the money, or lived anywhere near Atlantic City, my children would be living in a refrigerator box outside the Trump Plaza, because I would not be able to stop gambling. Thank God, I can't afford to go to Atlantic City that often. I really can see where this can be a problem.

Bob and I decided that instead of buying each other a Christmas and anniversary gift (our wedding anniversary is two days after Christmas), we would save our money and go to Atlantic City. He loves to gamble, too. I think he loves it more than I do. I think he loves it more than he loves me. I don't know why we don't just write "The Donald" a check and go home and sleep in. We always go with the high hopes that this will be THE BIG ONE. It always is. We are THE BIG LOSERS. We always leave the casinos with no money. At least we left the toll money for the ride home in the car. We do have rules though. When we go to Atlantic City we are not allowed to bring a MAC® card, the titles to the cars or the deed to the house. At least we know our limitations. We take enough money to lose and then walk the boardwalk after our fifteen minutes of fun.

I always start out at the slot machines. Mr. Big Bucks has decided that slots are a waste of time and it is only with his expertise at the Black Jack tables that we will become rich. So far his plan has not worked. He is usually broke within ten minutes and I find him scrounging the nickel parlor for nickels that the little old ladies are dropping as they feed them into Big Bertha.

My plan is much better. I always take the loose change we have at home, which translates into I rob the kids' piggy banks of all quarters, and start at the progressive slot machines. The jackpots are high and hey, somebody has to win. It is not usually me, but by the time I have no change left, my purse is lighter and I can make my way over to my true love, the Roulette Wheel.

Ah, the Roulette Wheel. My favorite spot. I like to just stand and watch for a while, and get a feel for the wheel, see where the little white ball is going to drop. Of course, I can now predict where the little ball is going to drop with the same accuracy I could predict the end of the world, so don't take my advice at the Roulette Wheel. But it looks good, as I stand there and wait for a seat at the cheap Roulette Wheel. I never have enough money to go to the High Roller Roulette Wheel.

As I stand there "people watching" I can't help but wonder how many of these people just have a lot of money, and how many are throwing their monthly checks into the casinos? For all of you out there who gamble just because you have lots of money and don't know what to do with it; send it to me. I will invest in five of the finest children this world will ever turn out, or I will take it to the Roulette Wheel with me so I don't look so pathetic.

Anyway, I finally get a seat. I pull out my wrinkled old twenty and lay it on the table. I look at the dealer, or roller, if you will, as if I were J. Paul Getty. He looks at me as if I were homeless. It must amuse the people working there when someone like me comes up with a lousy twenty bucks, when all around me people are throwing hundred dollar bills at him to get their favorite color chips. So now I have a reason for being here. I am not homeless. I am the entertainment for the person who has to stand there twirling that little white ball over and over just right, sucking the people in, making them think it is going to land on their number. And it does! My mother was right. The rich get richer.

Now I could play this game until a certain part of my anatomy falls off, and I will not get rich. I will have lots of fun, maybe put some new faucets in Ivana's penthouse, but I will never get rich at it. You need money to make money. I don't have it. Isn't life grand? I go pick Mr. Big Bucks off the floor of the All Night Nickel Palace and we head home with our tails between our legs, until the next time the kids' banks sound too full!!!!!

29
◯ The End

I wasn't quite sure how to end this, my first of many, I hope, books. I really wanted to leave you with some great words of wisdom, however I am neither great nor am I all that wise. If I were wise, I would check myself into a mental institution right now, rather than spend the next fifteen years trying to decide when "the time is right". So I will leave you this time, with what I believe.

. . . I believe in God.

. . . I believe in miracles - I have five of them.

. . . I believe people are basically good.

. . . I believe everyone is innocent until proven guilty, unless you live in my house, where my decision is final.

. . . I believe I will someday be able to pay my bills.

. . . I believe I will never get anywhere on time.

. . . I believe I will always get in the wrong check out line, even if it is the shortest.

. . . I believe my children will survive, in spite of me.

. . . I believe any therapist who takes me on will one day be wealthy.

. . . I believe all cars have a built in FAIL system, set to go off when you need the car the most.

. . . I believe people with foot fetishes need to find a new obsession.

. . . I believe no two socks will ever come out of the dryer together.

. . . I believe making school lunches is a "parent punishment".

. . . I believe what goes around, comes around.

. . . I believe a sense of humor is a person's best attribute.

. . . I believe God has a really great sense of humor.

. . . I believe I will never be done doing homework.

. . . I believe teachers do not get paid enough.

. . . I believe my husband and I will someday have an empty nest, and will no longer have anything to talk about.

. . . I believe I will never have a good hair day.

. . . I believe I will never again wear a size 6.

. . . I believe my extra chins give me character.

. . . I believe parents and teenagers will never see eye to eye.

. . . I believe pay raises will NEVER cover the cost of inflation.

I BELIEVE LOVE CONQUERS ALL!